You Can Society

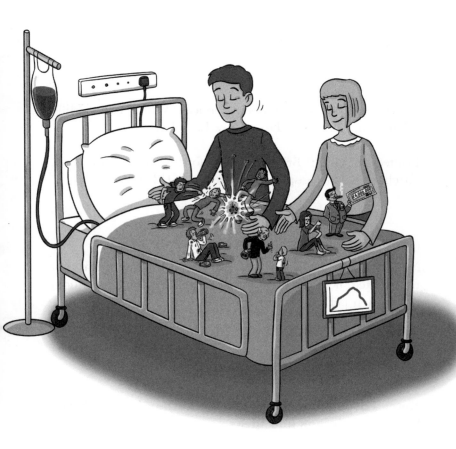

Alison Lea-Lodge

Published by Lea-Lodge Books
PO Box 447
Brighton
BN1 1SL

Text set in Baskerville

Cover designed by David Porteous Editions
www.davidporteous.com

ISBN 978-0-9548831-2-6

Distributed by Gazelle Book Services, White Cross Mills,
Hightown, Lancaster, Lancashire LA1 4XS

Printed in Great Britain by Ashford Colour Press Ltd.,
Fareham Road, Gosport, Hampshire PO13 0FW

**Note: Throughout this book the author is expressing
her own opinions and ideas.**

DEDICATION

This book is to celebrate and support all the right-minded - some 1 know well, some I have met briefly and perhaps only once, and many others, out there, with whom 1 have empathy because we all want to make our contribution to creating a happier and better world.

These wonderful people are not materialists or wildly ambitious in the conventional sense - they are good and kind, and are in harmony with their own humanity, and the humanity which can be recognized in others.

It is also dedicated to those who feel that their own lives, or the lives of those around them, are not as they should be and they want to identify and sort out their problems. Lots of today's ills are caused by focusing on a misguided set of values.

Read on - if you are stressed and feel frazzled as you struggle to hold your own or get ahead in the rat race you may find that ditching your conventional ambitions and settling for gaining a meaningful awareness of your intangible qualities – the real, human, you – may offer a loving and peaceful alternative lifestyle. Without any conscious effort the result of your altered mindset and its manifestations will be to contribute, richly, to making the world a much better and happier place for all.

I wish you well.

Contents

About the Author

Alison has had a variety of jobs in different parts of the country, and has a bolt-hole in Wales.

She was born in Luton, and went to school in St, Albans. At 18 she left home, and became a newspaper reporter first in Scarborough and Bridlington, then in Corby. This brought her into direct contact with both the local aristocracy and the criminal families who populated the courts.

Briefly she lived and worked as a director's secretary in London, which enabled her to have the wild social life she had missed while employed as a journalist often covering meetings in the evenings.

Moving on again she joined the Civil Service which, in those days, was a good place to be if you wanted a mortgage, and she became a commuter from Brighton to the Home Office in Croydon. She had a variety of jobs within the department, one of which was conducting interviews. Again, this involved her in meeting all sorts of people, from ex-prime ministers from foreign lands to those involved in squalid marriages of convenience, which could entail visits to prisons and detention centres.

Possibly the most worth-while job was her last one - as a community service supervisor. She enjoyed a good working relationship with many of the young criminals in her care, and got insights into the lives of youngsters who had gone off the rails. If only some of these kids had had stable homes and responsible parents...

After having a number of boyfriends Alison got married, late, to an older man. They were together for 21 years before he died. She does all-the-year-round sea swimming, digs her allotment, and produces and exhibits pieces of sculpture made out of a wide variety of things – what else? Ah yes, she loves classical music and animals.

Alison feels herself as classless, and is not politically aligned.

Introduction

I decided to write this book because I have found so may others who see things the way I do. These include friends, and also people I have met casually and with whom I have drifted into conversation.

I have been aware that we have all felt strengthened by our discussions. At the core of our unspoken and probably unrecognised belief has been the fact that the acceptance and expression of our humanity, which lies deep within all of us, is the most important thing we have both individually and collectively.

In a world which appears to be full of arrogance, greed, dishonesty, and violence we – the basically kind and well-motivated – make up the majority, and we must exert a strong influence in any way we can.

Often we feel helpless – situations appear to be outside our control. We find ourselves at the mercy of bad decisions and systems created by politicians and bureaucrats. These people have disproportionate power, but they are a minority.

We hate to see cruelty, injustice, and all sorts of other wrongs happening around us – but by getting angry and frustrated we hurt only ourselves. If we can do anything to improve matters we should do so but if not we should stand back, be objective, and understand how the situations arose.

Those who hurt others incur our wrath – but they should also arouse our compassion. There are so many people in the world who have been damaged because they have been denied the love and security of a stable family life and are deeply scarred. Some, despite sad backgrounds, avoid feeling bitterness or hatred and lead good, constructive lives. We must value them highly.

Whatever the challenges we face we must retain our own right-mindedness, identifying and rejecting false values. Far from making ourselves more vulnerable by doing this we become stronger. Knowing that we are living by the dictates of the humanity within us really does give us strength.

* * *

Heal society! Are you up to the challenge?

Can you tear yourself away from the text messages, mobile phones, and computers, and see whether there is anything written in this book which may help you to make the world a better place – both for yourself and others?

Is it even worth trying?

It must be right to do so. Our children and grandchildren will have to live in the world after we have gone – we owe it to them to try and improve it.

It should be possible to establish kind, caring, and stable domestic circumstances if we accept that these qualities are based on love and not material values, even if financial hardship strikes. This alone will give the future generations a great gift, and an advantage.

It is true that we may have little control over external circumstances. We must at the very least recognise and condemn events which result from the expressions of all that is worst in human behaviour. We must distance ourselves totally when the rich, famous, and powerful abuse their positions and inflict tragedy and suffering on their fellow human beings.

If we can establish – as I believe we can – calm and peaceful states of mind fortified by the strength of our own convictions – and the belief that we must try to do the things which we know to be right – we will be well-equipped to cope with whatever life throws at us. We will be one of the vast army of men and women out there, anonymous, but a powerful majority, who unquestioningly support our stand.

* * *

Let us, by contrast, see what results when those who lead us resort to extreme action, rejecting any feelings of compassion, and deliberately ignoring the fact that their decisions will inflict suffering on their fellow men.

We, the right-minded, must make a stand!

* * *

This book was written during the Blair-Brown era. The words 'the government' refer to the time during which they were prime ministers. They do not apply to the Cameron-Clegg coalition or to any subsequent governments.

PART ONE

ACKNOWLEDGING OUR SHARED HUMANITY

OUR INDIVIDUAL EXPERIENCES AND NEEDS

Every one of us is unique and should be valued. . . we need to take an objective view of our lives. . . how would we feel if we had other people's experiences and backgrounds. . . if we were very lucky or very unlucky. . . we never know other people's circumstances. . . those who glory in being anti-social with no excuses are not happy. . . we should not let them make us angry. . . Take heart – some people are truly wonderful!

If we are to heal society we must begin by acknowledging that all men are equal. At the most basic level this is obvious – we all eat, breathe, and sleep, needing clothes and a bed to lie on. At a deeper level we all need the same less tangible ingredients in our lives – the giving and receiving of love, doing things which give us a sense of satisfaction whether this is connected with our work, helping someone sort out a problem, or cooking a meal for family or friends. We also need to be comfortable with our environment, our homes, the roads we live in, the schools, colleges, and workplaces where we spend our time.

As human beings the experiences we have in our individual lives may be unique, but the fact we have them is universal. We need to accept this, and be prepared, mentally, to jump into another's skin to achieve understanding of that person's condition and experience. This is particularly necessary when we find ourselves becoming judgemental. We can never truly know another person's circumstances, the pleasure and the pain, the success and failure, the little things that hurt or give pleasure.

If we hear someone has met with a tragedy, like the death of a child, it will be very easy to make allowances, should that person behave in a way which we would otherwise find challenging. But the mental state of each one of us is largely at the mercy of the circumstances which surround us, and how each individual perceives those circumstances is unique. A minor irritation for one may be seen as a major challenge by another, and the contrast in the response may be tracked back to trauma, or absence of trauma, experienced earlier in life, or coloured by associations.

We can never know what is going on in other people's lives or minds. A couple who appear to be in a loving marriage may, in reality, hate each other and be going through hell. Someone who appears to be well may actually be at death's door. A trouble-free life may suddenly be overwhelmed by one of any number of disasters.

* * *

As we are all human, understanding ourselves helps us to understand other people. Take a few minutes to contemplate your own life, and possibly note down the good and bad things, also the environments you experienced through the different stages in your life – as a small child, when you were at different schools, time spent as a student possibly, and then in your first job, wretched time spent unemployed, whatever your life's experiences have been. Difficult – but try to be objective. Most of us have known some good and some bad times.

Now, as a mental exercise, bring to mind the most unlucky person you know – too little money, bad home circumstances, lacking physical attraction, cheated on by partners and knocked about, at best able to get a bog-standard job. Imagine what it would be like to be that person. Allow yourself – if you tend to feel hard done by – to acknowledge the fact that you have had a relatively well-favoured life.

Now go to the other extreme – and visualize the life you would have experienced if you had been the luckiest person you know. Lovely, wouldn't it have been? Think on – is that person, comfortably off financially, good looking, with good circumstances, and supportive family and friends – always as happy as you might imagine? Perhaps he or she is, but it is often the case that what the rest of us would regard as trivial problems get blown out of all proportion in the minds of those who appear to have little to worry about.

There is another aspect to this. How is the unfortunate one viewed by other people? With sympathy, possibly, though some delight in sneering at those who are not doing well, gloating over finding someone doing even worse than they are themselves. The favoured often find themselves the target of jealousy, or hotly pursued by 'friends' who hope to get favours from them. Genuine friends are sometimes thin on the ground.

* * *

Hopefully care and support will be lavished on those whose misfortunes are known although the actual cause of the distress may be unalterable.

But what about those whose problems – trivial or devastating – are not known?

I invite you to consider a few scenarios. A woman makes a scene in the supermarket, which started as some extremely trivial argument with another shopper, and which – because of her attitude – soon escalated preposterously and indefensibly. Onlookers stare, and marvel smugly at the behaviour of the perpetrator.

Now imagine what might have led up to the outburst. The woman had recently lost a much-wanted baby, perceived herself as a complete failure, and was distraught. Or she had become aware that her husband who had always sailed rather too close to the wind for her liking was being chased by the taxman, or that the police were making enquiries which could result in facts being unearthed which could lead to him

15

being imprisoned. How would she keep the family together and manage the children? Or, if older, she might just have heard that daughter had been diagnosed with cancer, and to be coping with great distress, fear, and anger.

Imagine that person is not 'that woman', but 'me'. At the very time when the whole of life appeared to be collapsing the sympathy engendered by the outburst took the form of judgemental stares, and sanctimonious comments.

Or, if a man, consider this. The job you have had for many years is likely to finish as the company is probably going bust. The lifestyle accepted as the norm by the wife and children is going to be shattered, and your status reduced to that of a worm. Or a few days ago your partner said she had been having an affair for years, of which you were totally unaware, and she had decided to more out. Or there had been a diagnosis of terminal cancer in yourself or someone close

* * *

If we are stressed beyond belief it will take almost nothing to make us lose control – the hoot on the horn from another motorist, an insult real or imagined thrown in a pub, criticism of a piece of work, almost anything can result in behaviour which is, in truth, thoroughly unacceptable.

So much for those who have been pushed beyond endurance. Perhaps if we see someone being abusive or aggressive we can hold back from being judgemental, in case there are reasons not known to us. Even if there are not we will be less disturbed within ourselves by reacting calmly and this will be of benefit to us.

* * *

Does everyone who behaves badly have a reason which would explain the outburst? No, of course not.

Still standing back, and being objective, we might witness a

16

perpetrator who delights in being thoroughly anti-social and unpleasant for the hell of it, driven on by anger and arrogance, often attention-seeking, and glorying in distressing others. Yes, such people are odious and can to untold harm to the innocent.

Should we condemn them? Certainly we should condemn their actions. But whatever their claims to the contrary, such people are unhappy at a deep level. Where is their humanity – the humanity which is in each one of us, and which needs to be fulfilled and expressed if we are to thrive as good, kind, well rounded men and women? They have turned their backs on it, and their lives have lost the most profound reason why we are on this earth – to express our love and compassion for our fellow beings.

Difficult it may be to do so, but we should pity these people. Their mindsets are a chaos of self-destruction, and while they deny this they are getting further away from knowing the inner peace and calm which is experienced by truly good people.

* * *

I shall end on a very positive note and in doing so illustrate how some really wonderful and awe-inspiring people do manage to put into practice what I have been saying.

Among the parents of the young and innocent 'wrong' identity victims of knife and gun crimes are those who respond to what has happened with sorrow rather than anger. Bringing up their own families they are conscious of just how un-loved and damaged are the youths in the feral gangs that roam the streets. Their understanding enables them to avoid being eaten up with hatred for the killers, although this would probably be seen as natural.

They set, for the rest of us, a magnificent example of pure and untainted grief, and bear their enormous and tragic loss with matchless dignity.

OUR HUMAN CONDITION

We are incredibly complex. . . each one of us is unique. . . we are at the mercy of countless influences. . . we have to determine what sort of people we want to be. . . but the true challenges to our condition are timeless – we are re-enacting the experiences of others over the centuries. . . the stories in Shakespeare's plays illustrate just the same challenges that we are all experiencing today. . . and that future generations will also have to meet. . . compare and contrast the results of those whose lives are dominated by selfishness and greed, and those who respond to their innate humanity by loving and being loved by those around them.

Human beings are very complex. We can be deeply profound or stupidly trivial, full of love or hate, buoyed up with happiness or drowning in a sea of sorrow, brimming over with confidence or trembling with insecurity – everyone of us has probably known each and every one of these states or emotions at some time or other.

As balanced people we have a wide range of responses to different situations and our personalities are largely identified by the way we express them. We are recognized through such patterns of behaviour, along with our talents and abilities or lack of them, the way we speak, walk, and generally behave.

So much for what determines how other people perceive us. Only we can know the people we really are. Even this statement is misleading. Carried along by the demands of our daily lives we have little time to give to relating to our deeper selves. We can live – at the survival level – without any thought for whether or not we are meeting our greatest requirement by responding to our own need to express our humanity.

We may well get lured by advertising and the media – and people around us who have been influenced by it – into believing that we are our trivial, superficial selves. We are not. In each one of us is a core of goodness crying out to be acknowledged and allowed to manifest through our care and concern for our fellow beings. The further we travel away from this profound and wonderful energy at the heart of us the more dissatisfied, restless, and unfulfilled we become.

If we could all get back to basics – the basic kindness, love, and decency which our human natures demand of us – we and the rest of the world would be incomparably happier. Have I achieved this perfect state? Absolutely not but I do know that I should be working on it!

* * *

An exciting fact – and challenge – is that we can change ourselves. We can take steps to make ourselves much more happy and content, as people, by altering our mindset. For some this may involve a relatively small amount of tweaking, for others a radical re-think of the way we are. I belong to the second group.

We sometimes view the way we are as though our characters and personalities were set in stone, which they are not. If we look back over our lives – even if we are quite young – we will probably be able to identify changes which have taken place. This is natural because we cannot help but learn in life, accepting and rejecting ideas as they present themselves before us.

So we are as we are at the moment, but what can we become? In making the effort to link up more closely to our innate humanity we will discover the inner strength and peace which is the birthright of each one of us, and a by-product of this will be that we become kinder and better people – and will automatically make our contribution to healing the world in which we live. And we will be happier.

I will give you an example. My mother was the most terrible snob. She was also very envious of people who had more money and possessions than we had. As her only child she brought me up to see things the way she did. For a greater part of my life than I care to reflect on I, too, was a snob, and did take note of such things as the desirable/undesirable areas where people lived, the professions they followed, etc. etc. when deciding whether or not I wanted them as friends. I really was quite ghastly! Thank goodness I stood back, took a long hard look at my mother's standard of values, and decided to reject it.

Some people, born into criminal backgrounds, are encouraged by their parents to burgle other people's homes, just like their fine fathers, steal credit cards, and attack other people with their fists or knives. Many of us have much to un-learn. What matters is that we do not have to remain stuck in the moulds our parents made for us. No living being is static, we are all evolving, and how we evolve is under our control, and no one else's.

* * *

Guilt and beating ourselves up over things we have done and regret does no good at all. The process of trying to reach a state of harmony with the better side of our nature should be seen as a healing. When we choose to treat other people badly we are actually giving way to an inner sickness – a sickness which makes others suffer but in fact makes us suffer more, even if we do not recognise this at the time. We are harming our own humanity.

See any change you wish to make in your mindset as taking steps in bringing about the recovery from an illness. That illness will probably have been brought about by one of a number of factors, possibly bad or inadequate guidance from parents or family members, pressure from an undesirable peer group – schoolchildren who bully others into acts of violence, dishonesty, or persuade them to become drug abusers for example – or simply being brainwashed by adverts on the TV and in magazines. We are all the products of our environment, but the big control factor is that we do not have to respond in the wrong way. We are individuals and can make up our own minds, and our minds govern our actions.

Sometimes people who have started off as good, kind, and honest fall by the wayside badly. For them, the healing may take the form of returning to the way they once were – or closer to it. Whatever the origin of our nastiness we are all redeemable – we can move on and upward to become right-minded, peaceful, and happy, contributing to making the world a much better place for everyone as we do so.

* * *

It takes enormous courage to address the issues in ourselves. Have we become dependent on meaningless external things? Have greed and jealousy driven us on as we compare ourselves – no, not ourselves but a totally false image of ourselves – with others whom we also judge by the outer trappings of their lives, their clothes, cars, and homes? Somehow we have to make the massive decision to reject these false and destructive values. If we achieve this we will be richly rewarded.

* * *

Escaping life by living it at a shallow and meaningless level will never be able to provide the deep feelings of peace and happiness which are the natural response to doing something really worth-while. It would take great courage and determination for the victims of the blot-it-out-by-drugs-or-drink lifestyle to take a cold, objective view of themselves and know – and I do mean know – that they are capable of better things, and take the conscious decision to change their habits.

In our broken society many people from fractured families have not received the steady, unconditional love from parents or the security of a stable home. They have been programmed to believe that life is hell and that they are not worth anything – no one has shown them the true value of themselves. But this is a tragic misconception – all human beings have wonderful potential, and somehow even those who see themselves in falsely negative ways must be helped to move on into positive and fulfilling lives.

There are many cases of, for instance, girls from terrible home backgrounds turning their backs on the old way of life, and finding husbands or partners whom they love, and making marvellous mothers for their children. Others may stumble across circumstances in which they get involved which enable their true selves to blossom – helping with a handicapped child, finding themselves included in a group of people who care about them, and among whom they can make a contributions and be appreciated for it – in all lives there must be – is – hope.

In deluding themselves into thinking that drink and drugs provide the answer addicts are just moving further and further away from the real solution, as they choose to deny the people they really are – human beings with a wealth of good, enduring qualities. They should link up with their positive potential, acknowledge and be aware of their own goodness, and express it generously.

* * *

True human values are timeless, as are the deeper experiences of humanity. Shakespeare's Romeo and Juliet illustrates the same tragic human dilemma as West Side Story – the musical greatly admired hundreds of years later – the love of young people conflicting with the wishes of their warring families.

On a domestic level in the twenty first century wealthy parents would not choose their offspring to marry into poor families, educated parents would not wish to be faced with rough and ready in-laws, and differences in race or upbringing present great challenges for some ethnic groups. But, surely, the love and happiness of the young should be nurtured. . . Chaucer's wife of Bath had on her handkirchief 'amor vincet omnia' love conquers all. It should, and if it is really deep nothing will destroy it.

That is not to say that love will not face challenges, and meeting and overcoming those challenges may prove a very testing time. Often a lot of tolerance and understanding is required, and patience. It is tempting to hope for a quick fix, but only something which makes greater demands is likely to provide a lasting remedy. This fact should not act as a deterrent, it should just be accepted that problems are a part of life and solving them can be difficult. However, if there is something we want, and know to be right, we should not be deterred from reaching our goal.

Shakespeare gives good examples of other challenges to our human condition. In Othello we see how excessive jealousy spurred on by insecurity in great love can have tragic consequences – particularly when suspicions are fuelled by evil and scheming troublemakers who want to hurt and manipulate us.

Whatever our concerns nothing can be resolved positively by excessive adverse reactions. We must stand back, whatever our own pain, and find out if the situation really is as bad as it appears. If it is we must somehow cope with it. I once saw an amazing example of this. I knew a man – I shall call him Tom – who was happily married to a very attractive and vivacious lady. They had two children he adored, and who adored him. They had a happy home.

In all this Tom was extremely blessed, for he had considerable health problems. He managed to have a full-time job in spite of these, but there was strong likelihood that he was going blind. He had previously experienced one failed marriage.

The family went on a weekend trip – some sort of social gathering event in which many family groups took part. The wife found another man – someone else's husband. There and then they each decided to ditch their existing partners and team up together.

This is exactly what they did. Tom's wife moved out, taking the children with her. Apparently she was amazed that they missed their father as much as he missed them. The matrimonial home had to be sold, and Tom, his health in further decline, ended up in a bed-sitter.

Knowing these terrible circumstances, how on earth could Tom cope we, his friends, asked each other. Tom must have been an angel, as he simply said, "All I can do is wish them well." I see this as a staggering example of caring generosity. I hoped that, when older and more able to understand what had happened, his children would see what a truly remarkable and wonderful father they had.

King Lear is a magnificent example of a stupid old man – but this could apply to anyone of any age or sex preferring the insincere adulation to two grabbing daughters to the honest love of his youngest, who admitted she loved her husband as well as her father. Putting ourselves at the mercy of scheming and calculating people because we like to be flattered can only result in long-term disaster – as it did in the play.

We should try to stand back, and acknowledge the true virtues of those around us. Someone who half likes us – honestly – is worth twenty who would fawn over us to their own ends. We must see through insincerity and guard against being conned by such people. Being let down is a very sad experience.

How little things change! Lady MacBeth is a superbly-drawn example of one whose political ambition and greed run completely out of control and bring disaster to those around her, and herself.

In today's world we see those in authority taking gross advantage of their position to acquire wealth at the expense of people they are supposed to be serving. They appear to be getting away with it. What do we mean by 'Getting away with it?' In monetary terms such people just about always appear to come out on top. But what must be their state of mind, the warped values they hold dear, and what sort of 'friends' do they attract?

Those struggling to make ends meet often feel jealous. Possibly they have far less reason to than they may imagine. These people may see themselves as abused underdogs – and at one level they may be just that – but they will be likely to have friends who love them for the people they really are, and who value them for their true worth. Often their communities, in their time of need, will rally round with a wartime spirit. If the wealthy fall on hard times their 'friends' often desert them, and they will find themselves cold-shouldered if their dodgy dealings come to light and bring them into public disgrace.

* * *

Can wealth and power really count for more than being loved and respected? Great waves of hatred wafted from the general public towards bankers whose greed and incompetence – for which they continued and continue to be rewarded richly – and politicians who further denuded the public purse by grossly abusing the expenses system, which they had skilfully designed for their own benefit.

These 'leaders' of society had conveniently – possible deliberately – taken the view that they were superior beings entitled to have whatever they wanted. Sadly, for them, what they wanted were the things that were meaningless in real, human terms. We could all see what sort of people were prepared to glorify themselves by greedily cheating us and our country – and we wanted rid of them.

Stand back – are these people you really want to envy?

* * *

In one of his books Graham Greene makes the observation that if you take the trouble to really look into another person's face you will see the humanity behind it.

I invite you to look deeply into two opposing faces. One is of a 'successful' person, who has achieved fame and fortune in a materialistic sense by elbowing his or her way to the top by damaging whoever got in the way. Self-interest was the only motivation. Greed, dishonesty, violence, any means were acceptable if the result was self-glorification.

This face is hard. It is without warmth, love or compassion, and illustrates the damage done – self-inflicted – by turning away from the innate humanity which is the birthright of all. All that can be seen is nastiness. Or is it? If you look more deeply you will see the struggling, pained, suppressed embryo of what should have been allowed to develop into goodness lurking, suppressed, behind the eyes. It is that presence which means that the wearer of this face knows no true happiness – only a sense of triumph at getting one over other people.

Now look into the opposite type of face – warm, happy, comfortable in relating to his or her fellow men, ready to help, a kindness radiating forth which invites others to give help in their turn. Success is not to be measured in material terms – hopefully there will be enough financial reward to ensure warmth, food, clothing, and a secure home – but that represents just the background for a meaningful life which expresses humanity and care. Here is openness and honesty someone trustworthy and everybody's friend.

At a deep level the first face is in a state of dissatisfaction and turmoil, while the second knows peace and contentment. Don't be tempted by the popular, false values of today to envy the first. Know, appreciate, and line up with the second.

WE ALL POSESS INATE
HUMAN GOODNESS

If we deny our humanity by following the uncaring mob we suffer. . . there is no deep satisfaction to be found in following the anti-social crowd. . . we are denying the expression of our true selves, our innate humanity. . . lives can be turned around. . . those without such problems need to understand the suffering of those who cause great suffering to others as they damage themselves even more. . . breaking out of this pattern is a huge challenge. . . if we find ourselves in a position to, we must try to help.

Many people's minds are in turmoil because they are pandering to external pressures which encourage them to behave badly. In conforming to the behaviour of the mob and therefore appearing to be leading satisfactory lives they are turning away from doing things that would give them genuine happiness and lasting satisfaction.

Spending more than is appropriate on flashy clothing to out-do those around them, making nasty but well-received jokes about the vulnerable, getting noisily drunk to keep up with the lads – these are just a few of the countless ways that people may feel they have to behave in order to keep in with the crowd. It takes a lot of courage to buck the trend, to stand apart, and lead a life which one feels to be right and constructive.

Like attracts like, and those who avoid getting caught up in today's unpleasant attitudes and actions often have many good friends – friends who would help and stand by them if they had problems. While apparently having many supporters, those who succumb to excessive shopping binges, or the addictions of drugs or drink, are more likely to be surrounded by people who would shy away from any form of helpful commitment.

Are people who skate about on the surfaces of lives dictated by appearance and materialism really happy? They will probably claim that they are but in fact they are not. Facing up to this truth, admitting that all is not well, would be an enormous challenge – and one that many would prefer to avoid.

I think it is no coincidence that drink and drugs are probably the two greatest problems in today's society and both provide oblivion. People with good, fulfilling lives do not want to seek oblivion – they want to live their lives with a vibrant awareness, making the most of every moment.

* * *

The very fact that people, caught up in lifestyles that ignore the deeper meanings of humanity, wish to block out consciousness by resorting to drink or drugs is proof that they are, in truth, people with great potential value – in a meaningful sense. While not allowing themselves to confront the unsatisfactory and unsatisfying way their lives are lived, there is an enormous and profound feeling of despair, at a conscious or subconscious level.

They have an awesome choice – to desert the shallow existence which they have made their own, and the friends that go with it, and turn their lives around and make a fresh start aiming at a new set of goals – or to sink further and further into their own private hell of trivial and meaningless existence.

Sometimes circumstances come to the rescue. A wayward boy may fall in love with a girl and want to spend time alone with her, preferring that to the pub and his mates. Or a young couple may produce a child and, genuinely loving the infant, want to quit partying and spend true quality time with their baby.

If someone acknowledges that his or her life should be turned around and decides to take action there will be many challenges. The old peer group will wheedle – trying to lure the friend back into old familiar, though self-destructive, ways – or mock, sneering at the proposed cleaner lifestyle which has been alien. When I worked with young criminals any who had decided to give up smoking were taunted with, "Are you afraid of getting lung cancer?" This reaction – to try to wreck another's chance of lining up with a more socially acceptable, responsible, and intelligent way of living – is evidence that the mob are sufficiently vulnerable that they need to keep their strength through numbers. Deserters are actually seen as a threat.

* * *

Drastic circumstances demand drastic action. A clean break would take courage but be the perfect answer – a new job in a distant town, possibly. Those genuinely regretting addictions or what are politely described as 'social drinking', 'recreational use of drugs', or 'having a little flutter' for gamblers might well, if honest with themselves, see a greater problem than they have been admitting.

There are excellent groups where they can meet others who share the same failings and are also wanting to confront and overcome them. No need for self-consciousness or embarrassment here – everyone is in the same boat. And they have the same common and excellent bond of trying to put things right.

There is no shame in admitting that one has problems and needs help. This is an act of courage. Shame – if one were to use the word, which is not helpful – would attach more appropriately to those who could sort out their lives and make them meaningful in human terms, but deliberately choose not to. This is actually a self-punishing cowardice. And I do mean self-punishing – whatever harm and distress may be caused to others the greatest damage is done to the self.

How to shake oneself out of this condition? Dragged down

31

by the inner knowledge – conscious or unconscious or deliberately denied – that one is wasting one's precious life and achieving little or nothing one must call upon that inner knowledge. **'I am a human being. I have in my heart the capacity to be good and kind – to show love and a caring nature to all living beings. I am able to allow this – the real me – to shine through. In doing so I will be true to myself – the person I really am, and which my humanity needs me to be. The reward for treating others well will be my own happiness.'**

* * *

If you need to take an easy first step contact Alcoholics Anonymous or a drug rehabilitation group. The Citizens Advice Centre may offer suggestions. Contact, for instance, charity shops and volunteer to help, enabling you to contribute to society while meeting new and differently motivated people. Go for it. Have the courage to investigate, and see what is on offer. Do not be put off or accept defeat. You have value, and eventually you will be able to realise your potential – which I am sure you have.

If you honestly feel that you do not need to take any of these measures – and many, many people do not, their lives are good and genuinely satisfying in a meaningful sense – then consider what it would be like to live a life where all the human values which are naturally woven into your existence were no longer there. Feel pity for the rudderless ships of humankind as they flounder about in the sea of their lives, refusing even to acknowledge the sheltering harbours of loving and caring environments where they could weigh anchor and be cherished. . . as we all need to be.

* * *

Heal the world by openly admitting and recognising your

need to express your own humanity, and acting on that need, and by also seeing the tragedy being played out in the lives of others who cannot find – or possibly not even feel they can seek – the deep and satisfying happiness which a loving, caring, and responsible lifestyle brings as its natural reward, and by feeling sympathy for them in their suffering.

If you are in doubt about the suffering of the antisocial members of society, consider for a few minutes the numbers of drug addicts and alcoholics who commit suicide, feeling that they cannot endure living their worthless lives any more. Others will freely admit they want to return to prison where they find comfort and companionship not available to them in the world outside. . .

True, these people cause problems – sometimes terrible problems – for the rest of us, but remember that we are on the outside while they are trapped within their horrible lives. They need a lot of courage to break free – courage which they appear to be unable to find. In fact they could win through. Often it is their own version of self-esteem which prevents them from trying. They see it as depending on a show of heavy drinking, dishonesty, landing a good punch, while meaningful self-esteem has its origins in being honest, generous, and well disposed towards other people.

* * *

How should we respond to those who – for whatever reason – are living in their own form of hell? Condemning helps no one. We must try to stand back and see these people who make victims of others as victims themselves – because they are. Attempt a tolerant attitude towards them. You are right to continue to deplore their actions, but remember that, so far as their true selves are concerned, they are pressing self-destruct buttons with each unpleasant action, and are moving further and further from achieving the meaningful happiness which we all want to enjoy.

* * *

If circumstances bring you into contact with those who are intentionally hurting others and also – unintentionally – hurting themselves even more, try to feel compassion. Avoid confrontation and, if given the chance, offer a reasoned argument.

When I worked with young criminals their discomfort at hearing truths about right and wrong in a rational discussion showed that they were very aware of the truth of what was being said. Their problem was in finding the courage and circumstances to enable them to change their ways. Their bravado was unconvincing. Their inner goodness was screaming to be let out.

If you ever get the opportunity to help someone to escape from the self-destruct way of life please take it. Everyone will benefit – the person concerned, society in general, and yourself. Even if your efforts are not successful there is the satisfaction of, 'At least I tried.' It is also quite possible that the seed of a positive thought will have planted, and it may blossom later.

PART TWO

UNDERSTANDING OURSELVES AND OTHERS

THE FAMILY UNIT

As adults have become free to drift in and out of relationships so the stability of family life has vanished. . . children have no option but to suffer whatever their circumstances bring them. . . those not prepared to accept long-term responsibility should not become parents. . . the denial that responsibility matters and society's refusal to point the finger of blame at defective parents has had a detrimental effect. . . the ending of a relationship can hurt everyone. . . but children have little or no control over such situations. . . deeply unhappy and in a state of confusion some manifest eating disorders. . . some respond by self-harming. . . others drift into bad company and slide into lives dictated by addictions and crime. . . we should view these young people with understanding. . . on the brighter side there are wonderful step-parents and people who have the capacity to give love in great measure.

Today the family unit means a collection of adults or an adult responsible for a child or children. It tries to imply some sort of stable environment, a house or flat, in which they live. Marriage may or may not feature and there may or may not be a lasting commitment.

As the freedom of adults to drift in and out of relationships has become increasingly accepted in society their children have become their victims. Many would challenge this – it would be personally inconvenient to admit this is an inescapable truth. The mantra 'children are resilient' is much more convenient. Argue as you like the statistics that England has the greatest number of teenage pregnancies in Europe, and a massive problem with young people wrecking lives that have scarcely started with drink or drugs, flies in the face of protestations that all is well.

So what is wrong? We must first acknowledge that children are not resilient. The more they appear to be, the more is their hurt and confusion building up beneath the surface. This will probably manifest later on – possibly half a lifetime away – as personality problems, often difficulties in making stable relationships because of lack of trust or an early role model – or be earthed physically and result in serious illness.

Unless potential parents consider the responsibility which they are thinking of taking on, and feel up to the immense task ahead, they should remain childless. The only correct motivation for making a child is the desire to create a new little person you wish to love, nurture, teach in ever way possible so that he or she can go out into the world as a good, kind, well-informed individual well able to live a full and independent life. Pleasing potential grandparents, wishing to invest in someone to care for you in old age, or hoping to spawn a child in whose success you can bask in reflected glory should rule you out as being completely unsuitable. Be scrupulously careful with the contraceptives. Avoid your disaster, and that of the un-conceived.

What has happened? As late as the 1960s there was an awareness of the need for responsibility. When John Lennon of the Beetles fame got Cynthia pregnant with Julian he did what I and my peer group regarded as the decent thing. He married, and they settled down to what they expected to be a lifetime together. This did not happen because Yoko came along, and the marriage broke up. When Shaun was born to John and Yoko John told how Julian had become a young man at the end of a telephone talking about motorbikes – and John wanted to do better by Shaun. If he did not feel he had taken all the responsibility he might have done, he had an uneasy conscience about it, and was prepared to admit that, in some ways, he had failed. I regard this as a healthy attitude.

From this standpoint we have sunk to regarding it as unacceptable to so much as hint that single parents, or ever-changing step-parents – common-law step parents – might be the cause of the mounting and dire problems being seen in their children. In our muddled society political correctness – we must never criticize – and human rights – generally exercised at the expense of others – rule supreme. Decency and common sense have walked out of our lives, and discipline – which used to encourage us to think hard before making large and possibly disastrous changes in our lives – is regarded as old hat. We have left it behind. We have also left behind the tradition of the solid marriage, within which – with all its ups and downs and arguments – children could feel safe and secure. Many children whose parents have separated express an enduring wish that they would get together again – even if they argue. They feel the need to have both parents at home.

Now, mercifully, some people are putting their heads above the parapet and calling for a return to traditional values. We have tried the 'anything goes' regime and seen that it has had tragic results for many, many children. Also – let it be remembered – for many adults. A high proportion of parents are leaning on drink or drugs to help them through life. The freedom which society has invited them to exercise has resulted in great unhappiness. Selling and splitting the proceeds of the family home – or moving out with no-where to go – and separation from the children can be very painful experiences.

* * *

While at least one of the adults will have had some say in how the dissolving of a partnership is going to be handled, it is quite possible that the children will not be consulted, or their wishes ignored for the sake of expedience. They have to fit in, like it or not and, as the adults fuss over the effects on their own lives, should the children become unco-operative they may well be seen as being difficult instead of being deeply hurt and disturbed – which in reality they are.

* * *

Let us consider some of the effects which dysfunctional families have on children. Luckily some of these victims often down the line are articulate about their feelings, and give us a raw insight into the appalling suffering to which they were subjected by a completely selfish parent or parents.

In the same way that the young victims of sexual abuse often – and completely inappropriately – think themselves to blame for what happened, children tend to feel responsible when their parents part. In their muddled and damaged little minds they struggle to cope with their own perceived guilt.

This can manifest in many different ways. Eating disorders, self-harm, and disruptive behaviour are among the most obvious, along with seeking out companions who would previously have been seen as unattractive and unacceptable.

* * *

I have heard the theory put forward that an eating disorder can symbolize control. While circumstances around a child may be chaotic an obsession with eating too little or too much food provides a sort of safe haven in which no-one else has power. It is a compulsive diversion from the aspects of life which cannot be altered.

Bulimia, in the form of binge eating and then inducing vomiting or eating practically nothing at all, is also likely to mean that the sufferer has an obsession with his or her perceived weight. Girls, in particular, often see their pathetically and often dangerously thin figures as fat, and they will not be persuaded otherwise.

The compulsive binge eating which results in gross obesity could well have started off as little more than snacking on comfort food, which eventually became an all-consuming addiction.

Either of these eating disorders play havoc with the body's organs, and are likely to do enormous damage. There is no quick or simple cure – these are simply the physical symptoms of a much more complex and challenging disease, a disease of the mind, not the body.

*   *   *

Taken that children feel inappropriate guilt when their parents' marriage collapses the manifestation of self-harm is perhaps predictable. Huge stresses build up, and an awareness of pressures at home do not vanish when the boy or girl leaves the house, they are grinding away in his or her consciousness throughout the time spent at school. Studies and exam results will suffer and as the child struggles to cope with domestic circumstances relationships with school friends may also deteriorate.

Confused, and feeling rejected and guilty, and ill at ease with the previous group of friends perceived – possibly quite wrongly – as coming from good, stable homes our young victim may turn to a different peer group who have no expectations of a traditional family background. These tragic and vulnerable youngsters – often resorting to the strength of gang membership – appear strong and independent. Nothing is further from the truth, but despair will stand between the damaged child and his ability to exercise any sort of judgement.

Taken to the extreme these are just the groups of feral youths who, almost always by the route of drug addiction or drink, sink into a life of crime. Thieving to pay for their habit their lives tend to go into a downward spiral as they become further and further removed from the socially acceptable stratas of society. They are alienated, deeply conscious of the fact, and their hate and spite towards normal, decent people can spin out of control.

There may be little we feel we can do to heal these damaged people and their fractured lives. We can, however, stand back and again try to understand how and why they have become as they are. Blaming society is not, I think, realistic. The responsibility for these young people's condition rests fairly and squarely on the shoulders of their parents. Social services get criticised a lot, sometimes with good reason. However, we should take into account that they are involved with people whose young lives have already been traumatised – they are brought in only when severe damage has already been done. Their job is not at all an enviable one.

* * *

However, all is not gloom. There are wonderful parents and step-parents who adore the children around them. Some step-parents show more care and concern than the natural parents ever did. There are families where the father discovers that among his children is one who was the result of an affair that his wife was having unbeknown to him, but whose love for that child remains as strong as ever. The generosity of the human spirit can be without bounds. We must be heartened by these splendid examples of the triumph of our humanity, and have faith that many, many people have these qualities within them.

CHILDREN

Prams and buggies. . . the kindness and creativity of toys in the past. . . the harsh and destructive toys of the present. . . the denial of the shared experience. . . selfish and bad parents span all classes. . . very damaged children. . . those put into care. . . what constitutes good parenting? Love and guidance are vital. . . material considerations take priority over spending quality time with children. . . the dangers of peer group pressure. . . many excellent parents do exist. . . follow their example. . . but try not to judge harshly the unpleasant troublemakers whose parents have failed to love or guide them.

Over the years there have been countless changes in the way children have been raised. Here are just a few observations which I believe have contributed to the rise of an aggressive and out-of-control generation.

Every now and again one sees a photo or postcard, possibly sixty years old, of a baby in a pram. The pram or pushchair was arranged so that the child was facing the mother, or whoever was pushing it. Sweet nothings could be whispered to the baby as they walked along, and, if crossing a road, the design of the pram ensured that the little traveller would be facing away from the traffic, and often well off the ground and away from the petrol fumes.

Today the baby buggies place the children facing away from the carers. They are the first to be pushed off the pavement, and it is a familiar sight that the mother is paying more attention to her mobile phone than to whether her child is safe, or frighteningly close to the traffic. If most of us, as adults, were placed in such a vulnerable position I think we would be terrified.

* * *

What toys are children encouraged to play with? Half a century ago they usually carried a positive message. Teddy bears and other soft toys tended to be of medium size, soft and cuddly. Dolls had pretty faces, and there were baby dolls which fitted well into dolls' houses. True, it is just about possible to get these today, but more and more are dolls becoming little sex symbols. A doll is not there to play loving, family games with, but as a reminder to the little owner that she must grow up and conform to the image of femalehood dictated by the advertising companies.

There used to be far more creative toys – children built things out of bricks, arranged little tea sets for dolls' picnics, put puzzles together so that a picture was created or a three-dimensional puzzle achieved the desired shape or form. Today, with the accent on computer games, the message is often that one does well to destroy as much as one can. Targets are there to be eliminated, whether they represent people or things. Children are expected to take on the role of destroyer, rather than creator, protector, or nurturer.

* * *

Computer games are played in frigid isolation. In years gone by board and card games were chosen and then family members would crowd round and take part, with bits of banter, and the opportunity for a little chat on other matters. Today's parents would to a large degree regard this as a waste of time, or simply not have the time, for such relaxation with their children. Bonding is not something that happens just immediately after birth – as it is alleged to – it is a developing process, and must be reinforced throughout childhood, and afterwards.

Family games used to be played against a background of mutual kindness, even though there was the sometimes quite vigorous element of competition. However, there was the accepted fact that siblings and parents or friends had come together to share the experience. Computer games offer no sharing, no human contact, no interplay between human beings. Socially, they are totally sterile.

Games like 'Happy Families', 'Snap!', or others that tested skills to some extent, like shove ha'penny, or tiddlywinks, would probably be sneered at now. Why? Is it because they do not involve the 'taking out' (which means kill), 'eliminating' (which means kill) or shooting down or hitting – yet more killing – of little figures represented on a screen. If you are good at the game you 'kill' a lot of people. Well done! What excellent training for the future!

* * *

While such games probably do little damage to the ever-decreasing number of children from stable homes who feel themselves to be loved and valued, and whose parents encourage them by setting good examples as kind and caring people, those who feel un-loved and are insecure – and who have good cause to feel betrayed and angry – will view their killing games in a different light.

Feeling that life has been spiteful to them, the idea of getting rid of the people around them who have let them down, getting their own back on those who have been cruel to them, and eradicating those perceived as enemies invites a strong and negative symbolism into the computer games.

Must computer games be designed with killing in mind? I do not think so. Instead of slaughtering the player could save – possibly rescuing people from a shipwreck caused by a very heavy storm. The player could represent emergency services racing to the scene of a bad car crash. Will the police, ambulance, or fire services get there first? Will they get there in time? Surely dexterity could be tested to achieve positive and constructive ends, with the player ending up as a hero rather than a murderer.

45

* * *

As children grow those around them need to encourage them to feel compassion for others in their group, and to be kind and considerate. This statement, made in our time, sounds as if it has come from the Victorian era. It should not. There is nothing old-fashioned or new age about treating other people decently. It is a basic fact that if we are to express our innate goodness and humanity we need to be educated to see how our reactions affect others.

Bad parenting – parents who cheat on each other, fail to give time to their children, and cannot be bothered to find out how they are spending their time or to whom they are speaking on the internet – results in problematic children. These same children, if given proper guidance, would have been considerate and, unlike the loose cannons, confident in themselves.

I knew a family who ran a coffee bar. Among the customers were a group of mentally handicapped people. Often this group outshone the 'normal people' so far as good manners and their overall attitude were concerned. They were polite and appreciative, and anxious about the welfare of others. There was no mystique in this. They had been cared for by dedicated people who worked with them because they loved them and wanted to help them, who had guided them, explained things to them, and encouraged gentleness.

* * *

Some people should never become parents. They are too selfish and too irresponsible. I have known a number of teachers and the accounts of the damaged children they have taught are nothing more or less than domestic tragedies.

One, Lauren, working as a supply teacher, was given a post in a rough area of London. Coming from a loving and supportive family herself, what she saw literally caused her to cry herself to sleep every night. Many of the children were blatantly and openly unloved and unwanted– and made to feel that way. The phrase 'the breakdown of the family unit' was without meaning – there never had been and never would be a 'family unit'. These poor, ignored little urchins struggled for survival, batted about between adults who entered and exited their lives in a haphazard and unpredictable fashion. Lauren just wished she could protect and love them all – she could not, and her feeling was one of despair.

* * *

Do not imagine that unstable situations are confined to what are regarded as slum areas – they are not. Karen, teaching in a private preparatory school, said that the words 'Mummy and Daddy' had become problematic. Wealthy parents obviously felt they had the freedom to play the field with girl friends and boy friends galore to the abject confusion of their children.

One father, who worked abroad, had the opportunity to spend time with his son who was at boarding school in England. He preferred to play golf instead. The heartbroken boy was reduced to tears.

When I worked with young criminals one of the girls told me, 'It was right that Daddy had his girl friends and Mummy had her boy friends.' If they had not, and had given her some guidance, it would have been extremely unlikely that she would have ended up in front of the court. She was a very kind and caring girl, and had followed the advice of a 'friend' on how to effect a credit card fraud. Not until the police arrived did she even realize she was being dishonest. . .

* * *

What can we do to help these children with defective parents? If we have contact with children we suspect are not being loved as much as they should be we must try to show that we value them. A child who is not receiving kindness will be receptive to care and encouragement.

I know – I was a child whose mother did not want her, and I remember to this day my reactions to people who were good to me. Once, at a children's party, I had a nasty cough. My father smoked an evil pipe, and I had chronic catarrh throughout most of my childhood. The mother of my little friend took me to one side. She found a jelly sweet for me, and said it might soothe my throat. I could feel her kindness and concern. She loved children, including me. I basked in her presence.

Another time cousins of my mother were visiting us. My mother was concerned – expressed not very nicely – that I was not progressing as well with my reading as I should be. The two lovely ladies – both teachers who loved children – gave me a little test, and pronounced that they thought I was at least average for my age. Their attitude was one of calm encouragement, not hostile criticism. How I loved them for it.

* * *

Social Services on the whole do their best. Their job can be enormously challenging. Yes, mistakes do get made and some – a minority – fail dismally, but I do not envy them their task.

I would ask everyone who meets a child who is, or has been, in care to show great understanding, also adults with that background. Not only have these people come from families who failed them, but they have had to endure the sneering attitudes of most of their school fellows. Any who turn out well deserve a medal. I got an insight into their lives when I was working with young criminals – many of whom would have been good and rewarding children if they had been born into decent families. One boy said 'I love my mother to bits, but I can't get over the fact she put me into care when I was eight.' I suspect she was a prostitute, and her son got in the way of her plying her trade...

* * *

What counts as 'good parenting'?

Back in the 1970s I lived in a little terraced house. Because it was on a hill I looked down on the neighbours' garden when I was doing the washing up. The parents and children often played together, with the mother and father joining in their games and communicating with them. When I met the children they were a delight, well-behaved and interested in things. They had been, and were being given, love and guidance.

I once congratulated Jonathon on how successfully he and his wife Jane were bringing up their children. I offer you, the reader, his pearls of wisdom – guidance resulting from what he had seen as mistakes made by others.

The couple moved in what were then seen as trendy lefty circles. It was the fashion to believe that children should not be corrected, but be left to their own devices, and do as they pleased. Jon and Jane observed the families around them. 'You have never seen such an insecure bunch of children. We realized that children must have boundaries if they are to feel safe.'

Discipline is an ugly word in the twentfirst century, but in its constructive form it is one of the many ways in which parents show their love and care. Giving children freedom when they are too young and inexperienced to exercise judgement is no kindness. It is vital to explain why some things are right and some are wrong, why some bring about happiness and others pain, and why some are safe and some are dangerous. A child who knows why the guidelines are in place and sees what happens if good advice is not followed will learn naturally, and understand why it is better for some rules to be followed.

* * *

The pursuit of money by both parents results in far less time and energy being devoted to the children. I fully accept that the rent or mortgage has to be paid, and the family's food bill has to be met. But if the choice is between changing the car every couple of years, regularly re-vamping the bathroom and kitchen, going on foreign holidays or spending time getting to know the children, and investing love, care, and guidance in their upbringing, then opt for the latter.

Consider this– cars, kitchens, and holidays come and go. The child that you have created will be with you always. How the new person that you have made relates to you in the future will largely depend on your input in those early years.

Do you want to raise a family who are kind and aware, well-liked, hard-working and, in the future, good responsible parents themselves, and who will always love and respect you, or will you give other aspects of your life priority? You can choose, but your children cannot. Why should they care about you if you ignore them?

Having a child is a huge commitment. Unless you are prepared to mould your life around your family for the next twenty years do not do it. There is no need to – the world has far too many people in it already. By moulding your life I do not mean allowing a child to hold centre stage, but to play a full integral part in family life, as well as being encouraged to develop other interests, if possible. Leaving the upbringing to a succession of child-minders, dumping your offspring in front of a computer for peace and quiet, or being delighted when the front door closes behind him and he goes out – to 'do' drink or drugs – is not the answer.

* * *

Sadly peer group pressure from other schoolchildren is likely to make your job much harder. The influence of un-loved, confused, and disruptive children presents a huge challenge. The freedom they are allowed by parents who cannot bother to give time to them appears to be very attractive. It is actually very dangerous.

However streetwise young people may appear to be they are actually immature and inexperienced. Under the swagger and bravado they are very vulnerable. Some of them will crave leadership and this may lead them towards becoming leaders of gangs.

The invention of ASBOs was an attempt by the government to control the behaviour of those who make life hell for other people. There may have been instances where they worked – but it was equally likely that the wayward youths would see being given them as a mark of honour – attracting greater respect among their peer group. I am reminded of one young criminal I heard telling another in my community service group that he had been to prison. He spoke of it with pride – a sort of criminal 'bar mitzvah' – the achievement of reaching manhood. However, the same boy, a few months later, became strangely quiet and thoughtful. He had got himself a girl-friend, and was actually looking for work. The boy was no fool, and one could only hope that the possible advent of family life was the catalyst which would make him change his ways.

For those on the social downward spiral fraternizing with drug pushers may be seen as increasing their kudos, enhancing their power. They are on the road to a life of knife crime and possibly killing.

If the worst happens and they end up on murder charges society – quite understandably – condemns them utterly. But sometimes the newspapers follow up the story of the violent death by giving an account of the young murderer's own circumstances, and often there is a tragic and terrible tale of a child whose life has known no love, stability, or guidance. The loose cannon was not born he was made. Very often a strong case could be made out for putting him into rehabilitation to get him into harmony with the humanity which I believe lies dormant in him, though un-known and ignored and making his mother, mother's partners, perverted uncles, and other evil influences in his life serve the prison sentence.

* * *

In stark and wonderful contrast are the parents we see taking the family on seaside holidays, with traditional activities like building sand castles, playing football, swimming, and looking for fishes and crabs in rock pools. All children face challenges and problems, worry about schoolwork, etc., but the young members of these families who know themselves to be loved and valued, and have the solid backing to two parents giving them a stable home, will be able to weather almost any external storms.

I have seen good family units beavering away together on allotments where children can get good healthy exercise, and learn a great deal about the wildlife they will come across, and how to grow a wide variety of plants. And healthy food grown by the children themselves is far more likely to tempt them than the boring fruit and vegetables which come off the supermarket shelf!

Herein lies the solution for those wanting to be parents and to make a good job of it. Look around and see how fathers and mothers attended by children who are well-behaved, well mannered, and interested in and concerned about all kinds of things, are relating to them.

Most importantly they will love them – and love them for the right reasons. At the same time they will be teaching them how important it is to be aware of other people and the environment generally. There will be necessary discipline – rules which are there for the good of everyone, and which, being fully explained to the children, are understood by them to be perfectly reasonable.

One challenge will be seeing the bad behaviour of children who are allowed to do as they please – a freedom denied those carefully nurtured and possibly a cause for envy and discontent. Again, explaining and reasoning with children will have to provide the solution. Often the loose cannons go too far – and the boys and girls who have been taught to think will see the undesirable results of the attitudes and actions of these uncontrolled members of their peer group.

Along with this must go an extra understanding – that the children who have more freedom may have parents who do not care, or cannot be bothered to give them guidance. Some of these will end up being completely out of control, and become criminal at a very early age.

However, if we are to live in a world with such problems without becoming angry and hostile ourselves, we must stand back, and see the history which made these extremely unattractive and often dangerous children the way they are. Viewing them with compassion and, if we have any direct contact with them, trying to give them a sense of self-worth – which will be lacking because of their parents' failings – we might be able to instil some hope into what tragically they may perceive to be hopeless lives.

EDUCATION

The problems faced by schools... untrained children... no possibility of exercising discipline... violent parents... how can we cope...? Adolescents are vulnerable... they need role models and heroes... they express themselves through their clothes... in the past punishments were seen as fair and reasonable... now children are allowed to be 'cool' even if their behaviour puts them in danger... no-one is supposed to be allowed to fail... can failing schools really be turned around...? Yes there are shining examples... are some degree courses worth the effort...? What about declining standards and the attitude of students generally...? Some really appreciate it when they are given opportunities... at the end of the day the parents have the greatest influence.

Neglect and inattention by some of today's parents mean that a few children are not even 'potty-trained' when they start school. Others have been introduced to letters and numbers, and may be able to read and write a little.

For everyone school is a big step in their lives, and they need to get off to a good start. Social skills, understanding that they are there to learn, and a willingness to do what the teacher asks are necessary if the early classes are to run smoothly. This pre-school training is down to the parents – and blaming deficiencies on childminders – childminders they chose – is not an option.

* * *

Teachers can be at the mercy of little demons. But these infants were not born as monsters – it is the home environment and the nature of the parents which has made them develop in this way. What of those parents?

I know of a school in a relatively good area. True, the

intake may be more mixed, but all the pupils are well fed, have neat clothing, and show no obvious signs of deprivation. Identified by their uniform one group of thugs from this school spent their lunch break hurling stones at people working on a nearby allotment. One holder went to see the headmaster. He was told that if the school had to call parents in because their child was behaving so badly there had to be two teachers present – because of the threat of violence from the parents.

What can be done about such situations? The parents are not of the sort that can easily be reasoned with, and their children are being reared in a very undesirable environment through no fault of their own. The government's and Europe's rules and regulations prevent teachers from imposing all but the mildest form of discipline. They are powerless.

* * *

What attitude should we take to these ghastly parents and their ghastly children? The fact is that they are there in society – our society – and what cannot be cured must be endured. Somehow, if we are to do our bit and try to calm the situation, we have to become as patient and tolerant as angels.

I suspect that if we knew the backgrounds of the parents we would understand them very much better. They are probably clones of their own parents, coming from angry and unstable homes. There will have been no steady role models offering love and security. Education will have been seen as a waste of time, and will have been sneered at. Money will probably always have been tight – with benefits and ill-gotten gains swiftly vanishing into drink, drugs, cigarettes, and gambling.

Those who have been reared by kind and caring parents will have no conception of the gulf between their backgrounds and that of the unfortunate – and thoroughly disliked – ones. Regarding these damaged people with ill-disguised revulsion is simply hardening their attitudes towards themselves as the outcasts of society. However loud and arrogant they may appear to be there is a very strong likelihood that their attack is the best means of defence approach masks their enraged and impotent feelings of inferiority. We can at least be glad we are not in their shoes, and not rise to the bait if they become challenging and aggressive.

And what of their children? Raised in an atmosphere of bitter resentment, and indoctrinated with the idea that they are right and the rest of the world is the enemy – unfairly favoured, snobbish, and to be opposed in every possible situation – their chances of relating normally to average, decent people has been denied them from birth. These damaged little people, like their parents, should be viewed with as much compassion as possible. Difficult it may be, but if the more favoured pupils in their classes – while not being adversely influenced themselves – could be more accepting of them it could do no harm.

* * *

At the time of puberty and during their teenage years boys and girls are extremely impressionable. They may be very unattractive and aware of it – with spots and breaking voices as their hormones kick in. They are trying to find their new, approaching-adulthood identity. Relationships with the family and peer group may feel insecure. They need props and heroes.

When I was a kid we had the Beetles and the Rolling Stones. No matter how rejected or ugly we felt, we could put posters of John, Paul, George, and Ringo up in the bedroom and drool over them. They had such great messages, 'All you need is love,' 'I want to hold your hand', and the Stones' rather dangerous, 'I just want to make love to you.' Brill. Joy.

Love. Happiness. All was positive and hopeful.

Today rap has entered the scene. No longer are joy, love, and happiness extolled – these have been replaced with tales of woe. Power and violence are glorified – there is a negative message.

* * *

In my day daring brightly-coloured mini-skirts became the rage, seen to be fun and challenging. A friend of mine once remarked that she felt that young people should not just want to wear black. Is colour or lack of it in the clothes we wear symptomatic of how we see ourselves, our lives, and the world we live in? Are hoodies favoured because they enable their wearers to hide away, cringing away from the world – a world they want to be separated from? Have they any optimism left?

Being a teenager can be a very uncomfortable time. I see groups of stupid giggling thoughtless girls and boorish uncouth lads and wish they were not there. If I am honest, they remind me of the horrible adolescent which I once was!

Memories of this time should help us to give all the support we can to the moody, uncommunicative, and surly young people that we meet. With luck and encouragement this oh-so-unattractive-stage will soon be left behind. We should also be aware that these kids are no more happy with the way they are than we are in having to cope with it. We are older and wiser, however, and should be able to understand their condition, and show patience.

* * *

Around 1920 my father came home from school, and announced that he had been caned. The family's response was, 'What for?' He had run into the road without looking and when punishing him his teacher had said, 'Your mother would rather you had the cane than a funeral.' The fact the story was still going strong many decades later indicated not criticism of the teacher, but an acknowledgement of her common sense. The little fellow accepted his mistake and learnt not do it again.

While 'health' and 'safety' are two words that tend to evoke groans throughout society parents give in to children who want to be cool by riding bicycles without lights, skateboarding down busy hills, and generally putting themselves and others in danger. We are in a stupid society.

* * *

Our stupidity knows no bounds. Over the years, to try to cover up for ever-lowering academic standards, examination papers have got more and more easy, and pass marks lower and lower. Children expected to get A* grades in their GCSE maths today could not begin to answer the examination papers in arithmetic presented to 11 + candidates in the 1950s. Spelling and grammar are seen as no longer needed – but they enable us to communicate accurately with each other, and surely that is important.

The rot has been there for decades but has got progressively worse. The politically correct idea that no-one should fail, and everyone stay on in academic education is nonsense. Children who are not academic will have some abilities, and those should be encouraged and valued to the full. We need bricklayers, people to collect our recycling bins, and clean the streets. These jobs should be given the value they deserve – we are all part of the same society, and we are all dependent on each other.

Some children are denied the opportunity of a decent education through no fault of their own or their parents. They have found themselves condemned to attending bog-standard schools.

Are we to see the situation as hopeless? We must not and we

need not. If a disastrously failing school finds itself with a dynamic and determined headmaster, and he has a dedicated staff prepared to give their jobs their all, miracles can happen.

During my early days a as newspaper reporter I had to visit one such school. In the 1960s problems with non-English speaking pupils were few and far between, but in the days when the majority of children lived with their birth parents whose marriages subsisted, the pupils in this school knew little of such security.

I cannot remember the exact figures, but a very high percentage did not know who their fathers were, or they were absent, and most of the absentees were in prison. At that time drugs would have been a less common offence than burglary or crimes of violence. The children who lived with both parents represented an upper strata, socially speaking.

The headmaster clamped down on discipline. No-one complained about the occasional clip round the ear at that time, but you can rest assured no injuries resulted. Then he made the wearing of uniform compulsory. No matter how poor the parents this was the rule, and it had to be followed. This did away with any distinction in dress between the better off and the least favoured of the children. If a pupil was supposed to be in class that was where he must be – not wandering round the school. Sometimes the head would patrol it himself. This was partly to prevent pupils stealing any money that might have been left in jackets or coats in the cloakrooms.

The classrooms were places of diligent study, and the children learnt. The system worked and these young people from classical no-hope backgrounds were able to go out into the world with examination successes to help them on their way.

* * *

Can what was possible in the 1960s be achieved today? Yes.

In a town in Bedfordshire a man was given complete charge of two terribly failing schools under a new City Academy project. Within a year both had been transformed.

Like the headmaster in the 1960s he made uniform compulsory and for the same reasons – and bullying was substantially reduced. Interestingly, it appears that rather unusual measures worked well – and I think I can guess why they did.

From 7.30am onwards breakfasts were offered to the children – and about half the pupils took advantage of this. My thoughts here are that there were probably a lot of families where no-one bothered about food first thing in the morning. Boys and girls may well have left home and, possibly, stuffed chocolate bars or crisps on their way to school which might well have resulted in a degree of hyperactivity in some of them. If they did not, then hunger would debilitate them.

The absence of meals round the table at home would have been compensated for by the companionship of eating with school friends, and this would bring about a natural bonding which would be a happy experience. They would be in a more benevolent and receptive frame of mind as they went to their first classes.

Lessons were also offered in the evenings and on Saturdays. To those who did not have pleasant situations at home school was probably a welcome escape. Also, boredom is a killer. To be surrounded by ones friends and given something to do would have been a welcome relief. These kids would have scarcely noticed that they were learning – and learning well.

Within a year exam results had been transformed. Amazingly – taking account of the academic history of the school – no-one left without a GCSE pass, and while in the previous year only 48% passed five or more subjects, this figure rose to 93% after the schools were totally re-managed, and truly dedicated teachers gave their all to the project – a project which resulted in a culture of discipline emerging naturally.

* * *

What about those who are seen as successful by going to university? I shall consider two groups. Those who, some years back, would not have been regarded as clever enough will either tend to struggle or – having got a degree – find that the worthless subject they have studied does not help them to get a job. I have great sympathy with these people. They have been conned and misled by the system. Had they got practical training they could have fitted in to solid, satisfying jobs, and felt much more fulfilled.

Indeed there were so many drop outs from degree courses that in some cases diplomas were created so that students could bow out with some form of qualification. Another reason for this was the Blair government's obsession with statistics. If a university had drop outs it was 'bad'. Conversely, universities that awarded first class degrees were 'good', so tutors were tempted to lower standards, thus making the thing meaningless. But you could not altogether blame them – the government held the purse strings.

I also have sympathy for those who were genuinely exceptionally bright. For them the course work failed to stretch them mentally, and they were unable to demonstrate their abilities to the full.

Again, we are at the mercy of systems not of our making. The only way to cope with this is to hold firm to the belief that students will come through the system – often in spite of it – and find their way into work for which they are suitable. Here, lack of discipline will work against them. The culture that young people should choose what they do, and not tackle anything they find unattractive, is a stumbling block.

In fact people are much happier if they are doing something useful even if they would rather be doing something else. Long-term unemployment becomes a habit so that eventually healthy young people are not even capable to getting themselves out of bed in the morning, let alone arriving for a possible job on time.

* * *

Let us take a look at the history of declining standards. In the 1960s getting into a teachers' training college was not necessarily very demanding – but at least those candidates had probably had the benefit of going to reasonably good schools themselves, and been taught by competent teachers. As the standards in schools declined so did the quality, academically speaking, of those wanting to become teachers. With the best will in the world, they were at a disadvantage.

By the 1980s there were schools that felt it was wrong to correct the English, spelling etc. of a child over the age of, possibly, ten. A friend of mine found her son's schoolbooks corrected so that his right work was over-ruled by the teacher's wrong. Where do you go from there?

Medical students – the doctors of the future – have generally been regarded as among the elite. Elisabeth, who had been working as an optometrist, decided to return to university and become a doctor. She was horrified at how the attitude of the undergraduates had deteriorated in the fifteen years since she took her degree. The medical men of the future would drift in to lectures late, mobile phones glued to their ears, and showing no respect for their tutors and little interest in their lectures. In medicine and in all subjects the country desperately needs really dedicated professionals who have both the desire and aptitude to excel.

* * *

While one can do little about the system or the peer group, I believe that once again the early training instilled into children by their parents holds the key. Conscientious and hard working, these qualities are seen as normal, and are taken for granted in these families. The result is that the up-and-coming generation will enjoy enough success to have satisfying lives. Even if not very talented they will do reasonably well, and any who naturally excel will become high flyers and provide the country with the dedicated specialists it must have if it is to keep pace with the rest of the world. Predictably, the academic standards of our children have slipped behind that of many being educated in other countries.

The almost miraculous way in which terribly failing schools can be turned round has already been described. How do some of the pupils react? Extremely positively. One whose eloquence was not quite matched by his grammar (no fault of his, and I felt hope for the future), said of the school's new attitude, 'It makes you look at things different.' He went on to say that if he was given detention the reason was explained, and the work he did during the detention could be a positive thing.

* * *

The truth of the matter is that if adults are prepared to engage with growing boys and girls, to talk to them, reason with them, explain things to them, and discuss things thoroughly the children respond very positively. Two levels of communication are taking place here. One is the obvious, sharing an understanding of a situation. The other, which can be more significant, is that the child feels valued. His views are being listened to and taken account of.

For children from good families in which parents spent time talking to their offspring this may be unremarkable. However, many will come from homes where they are largely ignored. Any views they do offer will be discounted, and certainly an interchange of ideas would never take place. To have an adult crediting one with having an opinion worth listening to is something amazing.

I had experience of seeing this when I worked with young criminals. On one occasion a lad described a film he had seen – and he recommended it. I went and watched it, and the next week told him that I agreed – it was an excellent film. An expression of utter amazement confirmed what I had long suspected – that while under the less that tender care of his single mother there had been virtually no communication. He was an inconvenience to be farmed out so she could get on with her own life.

A girl whose parents were endlessly preoccupied with their own affairs – affairs in the boy-friend girl-friend sense – used to take every possible opportunity to talk to me. I recognised that here, too, was a young person who thrived on contact with the older generation. She needed to discuss things, put forward her ideas and opinions, and share her thoughts.

* * *

There are many roads and areas populated with young families. Among these there are often one or two with problematic children – the ones we love to hate. Hating does no good. However odious the brats it will almost certainly be the parents who have created the bad situation which has arisen.

Tackling the mob may well be a non-starter, but if you ever get the chance to have a quiet word with one of these little monsters, do so. Away from the peer group, if you take the approach that the child is bright enough to take on board whatever you are saying, and that you value that young person – you may be pleasantly surprised by the result.

Do not expect a lasting reaction when the troublesome peer group descends, but the seed of a reasonable attitude may well have been sown. In spite of the bravado, most children, at heart, want to be accepted into decent society. I remember one of the young criminals looking at me wistfully and saying, 'Your friends are not like mine – they do not go around burgling people.' His voice was heavy with regret. A hopeful sign. He was basically a nice lad – which was more that you could say about his parents. His father had been so violent that his mother ended up as a mental case. So much for parental support.

THE WORK ETHIC

At one time hard work was carried out by willing workers. . . they accepted that it was right that they worked for fair pay and that this entitled them to a better standard of living. . . the bosses were much poorer then than they are now – they did not receive Mickey Mouse salaries and were not contemptuous of those working under them. . . skilled jobs, even if low paid, provided a sense of achievement. . . how can people cope with the mind-numbingly boring jobs of today. . . ? Now job security has gone – people are on contracts and feel no loyalty to their firms. . . from the customers' point of view the concept of service is vanishing fast. . . there is discontent and dissatisfaction all round. . . somehow we, again, have to stand back and look to our faith in our real selves – our human qualities – to carry us through.

People are quick to criticize the 1960s and to see the current rot in society as starting at that time. I would challenge this, and argue that the deterioration in the public's general attitude did not manifest seriously until the 1980s. As a teenager in the 1960s my impression of the England in which I lived was one of good and well-paid employment prospects. Plenty of evidence supported this.

Material acquisitions were becoming more plentiful, and people were keen to own new televisions, cars, etc., and to enjoy more holidays abroad. But there was the underlying acceptance that it was right that money required to achieve this should be honestly earned by hard work. Houses involved getting mortgages, but buying furniture and other items on the 'never never' the popular name for hire purchase agreements had quite a social stigma attached to it. If you wanted something you saved up for it. When the money was there, there was the satisfaction of buying it. The item was valued in consequence and, if manufactured in the UK, was likely to be of good quality, and last well. The idea that the country produced quality goods was a source of pride.

People in senior positions earned good money – good money by the standards of those days. Their incomes were chicken feed compared with the Mickey Mouse salaries, bonuses, etc., that are handed out today. I know this for a fact. Some of the girls at the school I attended had fathers in very senior positions, being partners, managing directors, or whatever in major companies, or medical specialists. These people certainly did not occupy mansions, or run fleets of fancy cars – they lived in four-bedroomed detached houses in good but relatively ordinary roads. While we might have been aware that these people were well-placed they did not attract the level of jealousy or the sense of injustice which attaches to their successors today.

This situation had another aspect – in being comfortably off but not seriously rich these people stayed in touch with the rest of society. While aware of their responsibilities in their work they also felt responsibilities to those who worked for or under them. Today the excessively wealthy appear to view those who make their positions possible with contempt.

* * *

I once saw a television programme which showed the original Mini cars being produced in the 1960s. In those days Austin and Morris – the British Motor Company – made these ground-breaking and excellent cars in Birmingham. What struck me decades later, when I saw the film showing their original manufacture in progress, was how physical and demanding the jobs at the factory were. The men were seriously active putting the cars together. The other thing that struck me was how happy they looked. They expected to work hard, and in return got what they felt to be good, fair pay. It was an equation they understood and accepted.

By contrast there was a film of the cars being made decades

later. The workmen, no doubt greatly aided by new technology, now played what appeared to be a lethargic role. They did not look happy – but thoroughly bored. No longer was there the immediacy in their work, nor were physical demands made upon them. They may well have felt their jobs to be the definition of tedium.

* * *

Obviously there is no chance to turn the clock back – even less than there might have been since the U.K. has lost most of its manufacturing industry. But somehow, wherever possible, jobs need to make demands on men's skills so that they have the satisfaction of knowing they are making a meaningful contribution.

An obsession with the snob value and desirability of white-collar jobs – no matter how boring or trivial – has undermined the respect that was shown to the craftsmen of the past. If a man could make a beautiful wooden chair he had the satisfaction of seeing his achievement, and seeing it appreciated by the buyer. Poor he may have been, but his work could give him inner satisfaction, and make him patient with his lot.

* * *

How do those in boring jobs respond today? Their work is a drudge and does not give them the satisfaction of feeling they have done anything worthwhile. Each day they go home, tired through tedium rather than activity. The only point in the job is the money they get paid for doing it – they feel their work has no virtue in its own right. There is no feel good factor.

This being the case it is not surprising that they start to get restless, wanting to get more and more money as compensation. They want their lives outside their working environment to be rich in up-graded kitchens and bathrooms, holidays abroad etc.

The decline in the country's financial fortunes which has resulted in many good, honest firms closing, and many good honest people finding themselves without work, has had the effect of making at least some of the dissatisfied more appreciative of their jobs, as they see others join the dole queue. Security no longer exists.

* * *

Again, going back to the 60s, and this applies to decades following that era, there was the situation that for most people, if they did their job well, they could keep in the same employment for life, almost certainly expecting promotion along the way. This gave them and their families stability. They could plan ahead, financially. The stress of today's topsy-turvy world was missing.

Now what used to be nationalised utilities have been handed over to companies competing with each other, and using whatever methods they will to draw customers away from the competition. Many a consumer has changed his or her supplier, and regretted it almost immediately. If gas or electricity comes from the same source it is nonsense to pretend that competition is of advantage to anyone except the owners of the different companies.

What of today's employees? More and more are on contract work – the employers' way of evading pension and other responsibilities. Some members of the work force find themselves endlessly applying, over and over again, for the jobs they have held for years. Others are assured that their tenure will be short – often so short that they will not have mastered the job before they have left it. I know of civil service posts to which the latter applied. Heaven help the public who wanted information. The system was at fault – with everyone getting a rotten deal.

Gone is security among employees, and the concept of loyalty is laughable. Having no regard for the people who pay them, if attendance at the workplace becomes too inconvenient because it clashes with a football match, then a 'sickie' is taken, without any qualms of conscience. This is another result of the disappearance of discipline and loyalty.

I met a student who got a job in a call centre answering customers' complaints. He had no knowledge of anything, and had to fob them off. He was someone I would not have trusted as far as I could have thrown him, but he told me he had quit because he got sick of telling lies.

Can we hope for greater honesty in the future? I am not optimistic. Failing companies are likely to do anything to try to keep or attract customers with promises real or imagined.

One can only hope that a positive spin off of the depression will be to force companies to become – in the long term – more honourable in order to survive. Sadly, many decent companies who had nothing to apologize for went to the wall, with the families of their employees suffering great hardship.

* * *

The English were never noted for being good where service was required – like waiting in restaurants. The Italians, by contrast, felt great pride in pandering to every whim of their customers. Now the concept of service is practically vanishing altogether.

The days of telephoning a firm, provider, or whatever, and speaking to a well-informed representative who could sort out whatever needed sorting out are just about over. One can sit for ages at the end of a phone, after pressing what one hopes to be the appropriate button as directed, and eventually speak to someone whose accent makes normal communication just about impossible.

Some supermarket employees are extremely helpful – but the policy from on high is pushing for the public to take over the check-outs themselves, which will result in – effectively – job cuts and yet more isolation for the population. A friendly word with the girl on the till has lightened many lives over the years.

* * *

How can we try to heal the present work situation? Jo Average has no say in how things are run. Where people have to work in mind-numbingly boring jobs they should make a conscious effort to take on challenging interests, not just go to the pub every night to blot it all out. Sadly, people tend to underestimate themselves, and doubt they are suitable candidates for demanding hobbies.

Voluntary work is always worth investigating. Sporting activities have breathed fresh life into many people. Going to an art class or teaching oneself to play the guitar – there will be something for everyone if there is the motivation to find it. Active involvement in something interesting can help to counterbalance the boredom of work.

There is another spin off – enhanced self-perception. It is easy for us to be dragged down, mentally, when we feel that we are caught up with a routine which gives no satisfaction and does not use our potential. If we can identify ourselves with something we enjoy and which we find challenging our self-esteem can blossom, positively, as we make progress.

Discontent among the lower-paid workers will increase considerably if those who own the company are seen to be creaming off excessively high salaries. Naturally there will be resentment, particularly if people are seeing their colleagues being made redundant.

In a decent world, where conscience overcame greed, those at the top could take a cut, to show solidarity and sympathy with those whose work made their own position possible. In some smaller, caring firms, such things may be possible. All too often, however, those in charge arrogantly and selfishly see themselves as above any form of sacrifice.

It is a lot to ask members of a long-suffering and under-appreciated workforce to stay patient in these circumstances. Unhappily, getting angry and bitter has no effect on the bosses and makes the underclass feel even more wretched.

However, some in these unhappy conditions weather the storm extremely well. How do they do it?

These people are blessed with an awareness that while they might spend a large part of their lives at work, this is not the most significant aspect of their existence. They have an inner knowledge that their true value lies in the sort of people they are – good, kind, honest, and caring towards others. They are comfortable in their skins, and nothing can shake this inner awareness.

* * *

It is easy to get caught up in self-congratulation if we are doing well. But whether we are succeeding or failing we must not judge ourselves by our pay packets, whether our bosses see us positively or negatively, or by the values which the rat race tries to force upon us. What matters is that we are human beings, and our real qualities are the inner ones – the ones which others can feel and recognize in us, and for which they love us. Nothing can alter these if we remain true to ourselves and our innate humanity.

If we hold firm to this knowledge the rest of the world will find it very difficult to hurt us – apart from at a superficial level. We will have put ourselves in the strongest position possible to weather redundancy or any other disaster which we might find thrown at us.

LEISURE ACTIVITIES

*There are many opportunities – a wide choice of leisure activities. . . -
which can be an antidote for depression. . . drink and drugs can be
disastrous recreational past-times. . . although they appeal to all sorts
of people. . . there must be more positive ways to occupy our
time. . . those who work to help addicts are taking on a great challenge
and deserve a lot of credit. . . even some of today's pop music is
negative. . . many are attracted to the internet which tempts teenagers
looking for love. . . and others with more sinister motives.*

There are very many ways in which people can spend their
leisure time which are healthy, wholesome, and positive. The
current awareness that we spend too much time sitting down
in offices and at home has resulted in a mass rush to join
gyms, go swimming once a week, play tennis or some other
sport, or go ten-pin bowling. All of these have the added
advantage – to a greater or lesser degree – of meaning that
individuals go out and meet people, possibly making new
friends and acquaintances. This is a splendid counterbalance
to our static and insular lives.

There always have been – and hopefully always will be –
drama groups and opera companies tackling the lighter end
of the music scene. Some community centres and churches
organize youth clubs. There are little groups of people
specializing in the same favourite hobbies – anything from
rambling to collecting coins. Some play bridge, or go to whist
drives. Anyone feeling bored, isolated or jaded should
investigate what is going on locally. Hopefully there would
be something which might appeal.

* * *

In some areas there will be a wide variety of night school

classes. These can be expensive, but for the older people the University of the Third Age sometimes provides a good choice of interests at more manageable prices.

For those favouring pursuits which are a bit more highbrow there may be classical music clubs – possibly regular concerts may be on offer – or groups for budding writers.

* * *

In today's world many feel they are suffering from depression. I would suggest that one of the best cures for this condition – which tends to descend if one is alone and unoccupied – is to be actively interested in people and things. Spiralling into a state of lonely self-pity must be avoided. Go out, join something, and become a participant. Do give it time – if you do not make a firm friend at the first meeting persevere. The rewards may make it very worthwhile.

* * *

The terms the use of 'recreational' drugs and 'social' drinking are among the greatest euphemisms in the English language. It may be true that some people can take the softer drugs regularly and maintain a normal life-style, never venturing into the world of heroine or cocaine abuse, but almost all whose lives have been wrecked by addiction started off by just smoking a joint.

Parents appear to pull back from exercising discipline or even giving firm and sound advice. Recently I read an account of how a mother felt she could not interfere when her son – a brilliant boy with what should have been a wonderful future and career ahead of him – got mixed up with drugs and eventually killed himself. Surely if you love someone and see that he or she could be starting on the road to self-destruction the right course of action must be to warn about the possible consequences.

The whole of life is a learning curve. Even the brightest among the young lack the experience and often judgement to know what is right and safe for them. A couple of men, good friends, and propping up the bar every Friday night, would probably counsel caution if one saw the other was about to do something silly or dangerous. Surely this would be an act of friendship, rather than criticism.

* * *

Alarmingly the bored middle-aged middle classes – very often women – are tending to turn to drink as an amusing pasttime. Some have admitted to getting into groups during the day – when their husbands are at work and any older children are away, possibly at university – and seeing this as the centre of their social lives. Perhaps this could be rather fun – for a bit. There is the hint of the rebel and the attraction of secrecy to brighten dull unproductive lives. But what of the future? More and more boozy afternoons while the waistline grows, the skin gets coarser and coarser, and the brain gets more and more fuddled. . . and possibly the liver and other organs start to pack up.

Women like these are not daft – they have potential which should be exploited. Filling in time before one dies by drinking is hardly an intelligent or fulfilling way to occupy one's life. True, people like this will probably not want to make the initial effort to get involved in anything meaningful – they have become lazy. But if they stirred their stumps and developed their motivation their lives could become genuinely rewarding.

Voluntary work, like serving in charity shops, might appear unfashionable, but it can provide a challenge and variety. Each day may be different, and the unexpected can occur. Staying sober and offering one's services as a driver taking patients to hospital for regular treatments would be very worthwhile. Any wanting to add another dimension to life should make the decision to find something to do – and not be content until well and truly involved in an extra activity.

If we are to change society we should ask ourselves if we are being fair to ourselves by making the most of our own lives, and then trying to encourage others to make the most of theirs.

* * *

What line has the government taken on the subject of problem drinking? Friday and Saturday nights are always a nightmare for the police and accident and emergency departments at hospitals. Resources – often strangely unavailable for other causes – are lavished on sorting out the drunk, drugged, and violent. Heaven help some poor devil whose heart attack coincides with the timing of the worst of the anti-social behaviour at the end of the week.

The 'solution' was to increase drinking hours. While booze got cheaper and cheaper – surely this was a perfect opportunity to slap on high taxes – more men and women could wreck their lives – and the lives of those around them – and their livers at very little cost. Possibly these people were seen as the mainstay of the electorate – the government wishing to retain their votes.

How to categorize different drugs, and decide which drugs should be included on the list of those banned proved another thorny problem. Many years ago cannabis may have been relatively harmless, but with the advent of skunk this is no longer the case. The indications that long term even mild drug abuse can result in some people becoming schizophrenic should also be taken very seriously. We are looking at consequences of wrecked lives and the National Health Service having to meet extra and avoidable challenges.

No two people react in identical ways to either recreational or prescribed drugs. The government should take the stand it must protect the most vulnerable – those who will become mentally ill but not know until it is too late. The nanny state interferes preposterously in many lives in many ways, but turns coy if it feels it might do something to upset another block of voters – the drug abusers. The most recent indications are that, if public opinion is seen to support a tougher line, the government might choose to go with the flow. . . and a higher proportion of voters?

* * *

If the government offers just about no significant solutions to our drink and drug problems there are very heartening stories of those who have pulled themselves back from the brink, and after battling most courageously have lived on to lead good and useful lives – lives enriched by their experiences.

Trying to help those with addictions is heartbreaking work. Those dedicated to their mission are likely to have to cope with many more failures than successes. No-one can cure an addict except the addict, no matter how much love and support are given. What keeps these helpers going? Some may have to get hardened to the work. Others will have to cling to their belief that everyone is worth saving – being given a chance. The reward of seeing even one person in a hundred quitting the habit, and moving on to lead a full and meaningful life, must be immense. A life has been saved as surely as a coastguard rescues a drowning man from the sea. Well done, those who help addicts. Keep up the good work, and do not get dispirited when things go badly, or be tempted into the ways of those around you. You are pure gold – keep it that way.

* * *

Kids have always had their pop music. We have seen rock and roll, blues, country and western – all harmless. Sadly some of today's musicians give a negative message. Some sentiments expressed in rap are quite horrible, extolling the power and 'courage' of the violent and inviting admiration for their acts of cruelty and degradation. They attract a very unhealthy cult following.

Such 'leaders' often have their own computer sites on facebook or whatever, where they are keen to show themselves drunk or drugged, standing astride the unconscious bodies of those they (and their followers) have attacked. Make no mistake, such attacks are almost never carried out by individuals. The aggressors are cowards as well as bullies, and without the support of those who hang around them would be pathetic and harmless – the damaged, rejected, inadequate members of society who have probably never known the unconditional love of a parent or a stable home life.

Their need is to try to compensate by making themselves appear impressive and important – and thus their savage acts of violence must be witnessed by others – others who by implication will become involved at the very least as witnesses and thereby find themselves under the influence and power of the ringleaders.

Along with the genuinely socially deprived may be some with more reasonable family backgrounds who, tragically and possibly going through the normal emotional and physical instabilities of puberty, drift into these socially excluded gangs, and find themselves caught in the web of fear – terrified of their newly-found friends, who quickly exert power over them.

* * *

Much publicity is given to the dangers of making friends on the internet – but it appears not to be much of a deterrent and there is nothing that many adolescents like more than defying their parents by doing exactly what they have been warned against. These kids are not bad – there is the natural curiosity which those starting to explore the world around them naturally and rightly exhibit, and the more naive they are, the more vulnerable.

Girls and boys still have the romantic desire to find Miss or Mr Wonderful – the right one for me. The pimply youths they meet at school, the giggling girls, or those apparently and terrifyingly sophisticated, do not offer much hope. Try the internet. In their innocence they see this as a possible answer to all their problems. Dream on, sunshine! People are people and while, hopefully, you will not get involved with someone who puts forward a completely false persona and whose desires are evil, you are unlikely to find some super being you can compare favourably with those around you. We are all flawed, and the key to loving is to learn to put up with the imperfect aspects of another person, while seeing just how wonderful the good bits are!

* * *

As we know the more sinister side of the internet is that used by those who have darkly sinister desires and who want to line up with kindred spirits – tainted spirits like themselves.

Before we had computers the ability for such people to make contact with others of a similar persuasion was very much reduced. Because of the nature of the perversion anonymity is essential, and this is what the internet offers, at least initially.

In years gone by a man could hardly have tapped another on the shoulder at a bus stop, and said, 'I want to rape and murder a four-year-old – fancy joining in?' We have invented a facility which opens the way for much evil, and well as the good.

There is no easy solution to this problem. All we can do is be vigilant, and to have the courage to report any suspicions we have. This will take immense courage if a wife suspects her husband, or a mother her son. We also know that women can be guilty of evil and obscene acts, and that many of these people live what are otherwise completely unremarkable lives – lives which give no clues to their darker sides.

ANIMALS – OUR HELPERS

We need to feel love and trust – but if we do other humans often abuse them, and we are deeply hurt. . . animals are non-judgemental and care about us for ourselves. . . materialistic irrelevancies mean nothing to them. . . even those who are indifferent to animals tend to be won over by their love. . . sadly some see posh animals as status symbols rather than objects for affection. . . and among breeders are some who see dogs and other animals purely as objects who will make them rich. . . children should be brought up with animals, they learn much from the experience. . . and a child with problems in life will have a friend to counterbalance what may be great unhappiness and loneliness. . . some animals are heroes. . . at any age we can benefit from the unconditional love offered by our pets. . . but animals should be considered in their own right. . . they exhibit compassion to others of their own kind and humans. . . and some are highly intelligent and aware. . . nature, too makes a contribution to our lives.

Love and trust allow us to open up the most wonderful and vulnerable qualities which we have as human beings. Fellow humans all too often let us down by hurting us, betraying us, or showing that they do not value us as we had hoped. For many it is the truly unconditional love which animals can give that provides what we need.

People are too often judgemental, comparing and contrasting favourably or unfavourably, adjusting how they see us and their treatment of us according to how we are performing in their eyes. We are constantly being evaluated and re-evaluated. We cannot take our standing or status for granted.

These may be harsh statements, and in some relationships we may be more confident of being consistently loved and valued. If we can honestly say that we are then we are lucky – and much more lucky than many others. If human beings let us down what can we turn to?

For spontaneous affection and lasting devotion a friendship with an animal may provide the best and most realistic answer. Cats and dogs have no knowledge about job promotions or demotions, scruffy or posh furniture, or any of the other apparently important and more materialistic aspects of our lives. They cut through all this rubbish, and relate to the real us – the kind and giving, the thoughtful and caring sides to our natures which it may be much easier to share with a dog or cat than with another person. Why is this? Because all too often many of us have had the experience of seeing our goodness abused or rejected. We have opened ourselves up, made ourselves vulnerable, and have been hurt to the core.

I remember once seeing a man who appeared to be sleeping rough with his dog – which was in a remarkably good condition. The look of absolute adoration in the dog's eyes was amazing. He worshipped his master, whom many humans would have seen as an outcast. Did those humans, or the dog, show the greatest qualities attributed to humanity?

Pets can win us over. I knew a lady – a divorced mother – who did not like cats. She allowed her prejudice to be overruled by her son and daughter who had seen, and wanted to offer a home to, a kitten. Within weeks the sweet nature of the little furry bundle – a very ordinary little puss – had won her over entirely. She even allowed little Katie to have a litter of kittens, and she bought her herrings and other feline luxuries so that she and her family would be healthy.

Few normal people who start off disliking or being indifferent to animals can maintain that attitude if they find themselves the unsolicited object of spontaneous affection. Big brown doggie eyes looking up with a wish for friendship and ready to give unbounded love cannot be resisted for long. A wheedling cat requesting a lap and rewarding it with purrs and head-butts – cats are so independent and do not care about anyone say those who have not a clue about them – is irresistible. We all want to be loved, and when animals show love it is because they want to – it is in their nature.

Of course not all animals are equally loving. Bad breeding or experiences before being rescued may have influenced the personality. As one who took on an animal terrified by the extremely cruel treatment she suffered in a previous home I can report that all the effort and encouragement spent in trying to heal Kitty-Puss were repaid a hundredfold by the love and loyalty which was my reward over many years.

* * *

The motivation for acquiring a pet is very important. If the animal is going to play the role of a status symbol, expensive and highly bred, I am very doubtful. In the same way that children should be wanted as objects to be given love, not born to answer a list of expectations, so should animals. Children, puppies, and kittens all need training, too, calling on a mixture of love and discipline which is essential in any home.

All too often stories of horrendous cruelty to animals hit the headlines – very often committed by breeders or others who see dogs, horses, or whatever as a part of their trade. While for most of us it is the giving and receiving of love which attracts us to our pets, for others these poor creatures are seen as moneymaking objects.

Over the years publicity has – rightly – been given to the fact that some dogs have been bred purely with appearance in mind. The face has become more and more squashed so that some poor dogs can scarcely breathe and suffer terribly in hot weather. The characteristic of Rhodesian ridgebacks is actually – like the tail-less rumps of Manx cats – a manifestation of a deformity, which has been exploited as a marketing feature. Some vets have agreed to kill Rhodesian ridgebacks lacking the ridge to humour breeders – although in doing so they are destroying the more healthy of the puppies. The more healthy but less remunerative. . . this tells us all we need to know about those breeders, the sort of people some of them are, and some vets.

Animals which have been used for breeding are often callously put down as they get older – and they begin to produce fewer offspring in each litter. Cases where unwanted puppies or kittens are left to die rather than being found homes or put down humanely are far from unknown – and almost never is any remorse expressed by the breeder. Many dogs used for breeding are kept in sheds. Some have never been into a house, have no regular walks, and have scarcely any daylight.

Animals are demanding, and it is not surprising that among those handed in to rescue centres are those that cost a lot of money. Caring for a dog and what is seen as the inconvenience outweighs the status symbol advantages for which it was bought.

* * *

I believe it is an excellent thing for children to be brought up with animals. There are many reasons for this. One is that girls and boys must learn to treat all living beings well. They must understand about kindness and cruelty, that one is right and one is wrong. There will be a natural balance between how a child treats an animal and how it responds – a very valuable lesson for the boy or girl – and awareness that we have a big responsibility to those who are dependent upon us for their survival and happiness.

We hear a great deal about the problems many children have at school. There can be great pressures as exams loom, with all the implications tied up with success or failure. Parents often cannot help being anxious, wanting positive futures for their offspring, and the home atmosphere may become increasingly tense.

As discipline in many schools has declined – often because

the teachers are not allowed to enforce it effectively – so bullying has increased. Children are often embarrassed if they are the victims, holding all the hurt inside, and feeling lonely and frightened. When I hear that, tragically, some poor girl or boy has attempted or succeeded in committing suicide I often wonder if the presence of a dog or cat in the household might have helped to avert such a disaster. To come home to a warm, soft moggie, take the animal in ones arms, and feel its love and reassuring purr, to feel the soft lump of companionable feline-hood nestling against one during the night. . . few experiences can be so therapeutic.

Equally, the enthusiastic welcome of a dog, full of love, with pricked up ears and a wagging tail, can only raise the spirits and self-esteem of a schoolchild having a very hard time. In that dog is a friend whose love is never going to fail.

We must have outlets for the expressions of our humanity. I would suggest that domestic pets can provide an answer to this need. Their love has the unconditional quality which is so often missing in human relationships.

* * *

How far will animals go in protecting the people who love them? Much further than many people, I suspect.

When I heard an old lady who lived in a big house – it was in the days when people left their front doors open – say that her cat had flung himself at the throat of an intruder who was approaching her I did not quite believe her. . . until I saw my own cat prepared to try something similar.

My father had a very demanding job and would sometimes bring home work, and work through the night. The cat – who enjoyed night-time pursuits – had discovered that if he climbed onto the fence he could jump onto a balcony outside my bedroom window, and meow until I opened it and let him in. This was in the dark ages before cat flaps had been invented.

One night he did just that. Unbeknown to him my father was downstairs, working. The cat heard a sound which he took to be caused by an intruder. He jumped off the bed, and positioned himself at the top of the stairs. I went to see what was happening. I found him tensed up and growling, while also trembling with fear. Luckily my father coughed. The cat recognised the sound, his whole body relaxed, and he came back to bed.

I love dogs and cats and they often sense this. Many a dog having his walk has come and greeted me. Toby introduced himself to me, a medium-sized mongrel who loved the world and was everybody's friend, or almost. I chatted to his owners. The wife used crutches, but walked amazingly well. They told me that Toby was a hero. His mistress had been exercising him along a country path when a man jumped out of the bushes. The dog, running on ahead, turned round and raced back. He sank his teeth into the potential attacker's leg. As soon as he let go the attacker fled. The matter was reported to the police, and the couple were concerned that Toby might be regarded as dangerous. Common sense prevailed, and the police saw him as a hero who had protected his owner.

I knew a tiny miniature Yorkshire Terrier that would set up the most enormous barking if anyone got near the baby's pram.

* * *

Animals should not, however, just be regarded as additions to our homes – they exist in their own right and it is all too easy to underestimate them.

Nothing could be further from the truth than using the term behaving like an animal in a derogatory way. They have their own codes of conduct – their own standards of decency. Some of us could learn a lot from them.

I knew a family who had a number of cats. One suffered an

accident which left him slightly brain-damaged, rather clumsy and inclined to get in the way. If another cat showed impatience or any kind of hostility to him the rest of the feline family would way in to protect the vulnerable one.

I once tried to catch a guillemot which had flopped onto the beach covered in tar. I failed dismally, and the poor thing dragged itself back into the water before I could reach it. Its only hope of survival – being captured and cleaned – had vanished. As the tide bore it away I saw an ever-increasing flock of sea birds overhead, encircling it, seeing its distress and trying to offer support.

Like many pet owners I have been comforted, when ill, by my furry friends. On coming out of hospital I found that my cat stayed firmly by my side. When my father, trying to get over a severe stroke, was bordering on a breakdown a different cat, who went thin with worry, kept guard by the bedroom door. He knew that my father could face no-one and just wanted to be left alone. The animal made sad little noises to anyone entering the room. Seeing the master whom he loved ill and suffering moved him deeply.

I heard a lady tell of how her rescued birds would show their concern if she cried or was in distress by landing on her shoulder, cooing to her, and generally paying her extra attention until she recovered.

* * *

Some animals are highly intelligent. I knew one dog that quite freaked me out – her understanding of the words of the English language were so much in excess of the usual, 'Sit', 'Stop', and 'Walkies'. A member of another dog's family who expressed irritation when someone left a door open and said, 'I wish Puck could shut the door', saw with amazement that the little terrier Puck did just that, paws up and pushing on the wood until the lock clicked.

One of my rescued cats – we knew little of his background

at the time – hid from us when he smelt whisky. We were having a little tot to see in the New Year. It took a long time for him to come out from his place of safety, and he continued to watch us intently. We discovered afterwards that his previous owner was a drunkard, and used to beat him when under the influence.

Some scientists discovered that mature pigeons could learn a few things more readily than a three-year-old child. An animal's level of awareness can outstrip ours. One day friends in America were very puzzled that the fish in their pond would not surface to take their daily food. That night there was an earthquake. By staying at the bottom of the pond the fish survived. Spiders are terrified of sudden light – one can see why!

* * *

Whatever we mean by 'creation' some parts of it are really amazing. I am blown away when I consider that a tiny fly or other insect, which could fit on a pin-head, has a complete survival system in its microscopic body. It eats, finds a suitable place to live, mates, and produces its young. It has so much in common with human beings – yet all the organs of its body are so tiny in comparison with ours.

Great pleasure is to be had in appreciating wildlife. Twitchers follow their birds, and many people watch out, every year, for the butterflies which are attracted to particular flowers. These little treats come free, and tend to have a soothing effect on us. They are nature's antidote to our often fraught lives.

Life And Death

Life and death are matters where we should be allowed to hold our own council. . . should suffering be allowed to continue to prolong life, or should people be allowed to ebb away...what about saving tiny babies who may be terribly handicapped for life. . . ? should the parents be able to decide. . . ? different parents cope or do not cope in different ways. . . what about helping the old and suffering to end their lives. . . ? each individual is different.

There are some matters on which we each have to make our own decisions and judgements. Sometimes they involve life or death, and may apply to ourselves or others. I think we should each be guided by our individual consciences.

Watching someone terribly ill and obviously suffering in hospital is it compassionate to want the condition to be prolonged, if the patient's condition is believed to be terminal? Or should we just wish them to ebb away? If it is someone we deeply love will it hurt them and us more if the agony continues for days or possibly weeks, or will death bring relief to all? Should it be welcomed as quickly as possible?

There are no glib answers here. Should we be allowed to take our own lives? What if someone very close to us wants to die and needs help, or not to die alone? This is no subject upon which politicians or anyone else can pontificate. Each case is, truly, unique. I cannot tell what is going on in your mind, and you cannot tell what is going on in mine.

* * *

At the other end of life – birth – medical advances mean that very tiny babies can be kept alive in a way never previously dreamed of. Sometimes the little survivor lives on to lead a full, normal, and happy life. Statistically – and demonstrably –

91

there are many who prove the wonders of science in one sense, but science offers no antidote for the extreme suffering that the many little babies with terrible handicaps will have to endure.

One set of parents went to court insisting that their tragically handicapped child should be kept alive although the doctors were convinced that that life was already ridden with pain, and normal activities would be impossible. The child survived, and the 'loving' parents split up. A life in a nursing home was the only option. The parents were conveniently away from it all.

* * *

Setting aside all political considerations I condemned those who criticized David Cameron when he said that he believed that the parents should have the right to say if a child, known to be severely handicapped while still in the womb, should have its life terminated with an abortion.

Unlike most of us he who had six years to enjoy the life of his very handicapped boy – whom he genuinely loved – was in a position to see what caring for such a child involved. It was accepted even by his political enemies that he had genuine experience of meeting other parents – none with his advantages – who were facing up to the challenge.

If the child is not just to be dumped in a home the implications are enormous. What about the effect on other or future siblings? How can a man hold down a job if he never gets a night's sleep? Can they survive financially if the mother will never be able to work again? Will they, seeing, loving, and suffering with their child, feel that the effort is worth it for themselves or the new life they have created? How can one apply a 'quality of life' criteria to one who may be deaf, blind, and unable to move?

I know of one loving and caring family who have such a daughter and she is valued very greatly. But I do not regard them as average people – they are very special and few could cope as they do. Also, the child shows signs of happiness and does respond, albeit in a limited way. But I know of another family where a child cannot even discriminate between the loving mother who cares for him, and other people. Heartbreaking.

We should avoid being judgemental in all these cases.

I deplore unreservedly the prison sentence of three years passed on the son of an elderly and terminally ill man, who begged to be brought a gun so he could end his suffering. In providing the gun the son, a middle-aged and responsible man, was offering the last compassionate gift to his father, the father he loved.

Imagine the son's feeling had he denied his father's wish, and watched him die in agony, knowing that it had been in his power to prevent this.

* * *

The last of my aunts to die was in a very good private nursing home. She was an extremely intelligent woman who had had a good career – she was very highly regarded by the company whose business she ran – she read the Daily Telegraph from cover to cover, enjoyed going to concerts and operas, and was a fund of knowledge and very talented.

Imagine – or perhaps do not imagine – sitting in a chair deaf, almost blind, certainly unable to read, in constant pain probably from tiny brain haemorrhages, and though not incontinent unable to go to the loo on her own. She had Meniere's disease so that if she stood up she felt dizzy and had no balance. Once when I visited her she fixed me with her one partially-sighted eye, and said, "I have had enough". I knew she meant it. I asked the nurse that if my aunt – whom I loved dearly and whom I would miss very much – got pneumonia please not to stuff her full of antibiotics, but to let her drift away.

She got pneumonia, was treated for it – against her wishes – and had to continue to live though, mercifully, for only a short time.

By contrast I knew a lady who had been in a nursing home where she spent her time – partly through her own wishes – in bed in her own room doing nothing. She refused to have music, a television, or books. This state of affairs had been going on for years, yet she told me, "I am suffering but I do not want to die."

We are all individuals. None of us should be so ignorant nor so arrogant as to think we can apply hard and fast rules in these cases.

A thought. I loved my aunt dearly. We lived over 100 miles away, but we tried to visit her about every six weeks. Frail though she was I could still feel the essence of the person she had once been and I loved seeing her. For my personal convenience I would have liked her to live forever. But I was not the one who was in pain. I felt that, by wishing for her to remain alive, I was like the Victorians who caught songbirds and put them in cages, where the poor little things would soon die. Selfishness overcame compassion.

* * *

Money is often seen as an issue – grabbing relatives wanting the elderly to snuff it so they can get their hands on the dough. Horrible! (More people who have turned their backs on their humanity!) However, money might even be the issue the other way round.

I knew a man who was diagnosed with lung cancer and was invited to start treatment. He refused saying that he had had a wonderful life. His business had been successful, the wife he had loved had already died, and he had the satisfaction of seeing his two lovely daughters in happy marriages. He preferred to quietly ebb away. His time had come.

I think it perfectly possible that, had he ever been in the

position he wanted to avoid, of spending a wretched time in a nursing home, horribly uncomfortable, useless, and suffering, he would have wanted his family's funds to go not into expensive residential care, but to be used for an enhanced lifestyle for the family he loved. I wonder if this has ever been a contributing cause of the suicide of an unhappy old person facing a bleak future? Unlikely perhaps, but not impossible.

* * *

I have no children of my own, but a goddaughter whom I love dearly. We have always had a very good and comfortable relationship – in fact she appears to have valued me much more than I deserved! Once, before she was married, she made some comment to the effect that she would want to help me if I needed it.

I told her – and while I am in my right mind I would always tell her – that I would not want her life or that of any younger person to be crippled by mine. I cannot foresee the future. But if I become senile, awkward, selfish, demanding, and possibly hostile to any who oppose me, I do not want the 'judgement'. I might express then to be regarded as that of the true 'me'. Please let me be known for ever as a reasonable balanced person, before the ravages of time have reduced my brain to a mindless pulp and my body to a wrinkled and battered apology for its earlier self.

PART THREE

OTHER INFLUENCES IN OUR LIVES

THE ADVERTISING INDUSTRY

Adverts appeal to what is worst in us – the trivial and superficial. . . and imply that without buying the things they are selling we will be failures and social outcasts. . . the pressure this materialistic standard of values puts on the breadwinners is immense. . . their families may value them purely in terms of providers. . . everyone tends to get caught up in the 'must have' culture at some point particularly the young and inadequate. . . those with no money get themselves heavily into debt as they try to keep up with the trend. . . However the truly successful – those comfortable in their own skins – can demonstrate that material possessions are without meaning for them as they understand that true value lies only in the deeper qualities which underlie our innate humanity. There are some wonderful, hopeful signs. Some youngsters discovered for themselves their true values by abandoning essential make-up and mobiles. . . while some invest fortunes in trying to improve their outward appearance others have found that part of themselves which really counts – have related to, and are expressing their true humanity.

The advertising industry plies its trade by appealing to what is worst in us – the most superficial and trivial. We are, apparently, supposed to conform to their pattern. Whatever our age there is not supposed to be a grey hair or a wrinkle in sight, and we should live in homes stuffed with the latest furniture, computers etc. and own the newest and trendiest cars or four wheeled drives. We are, by implication, told that if we fail to project this display of wealth and modernity we will be social outcasts despised and rejected by everyone around us.

The strength which this completely false standard of values has manifested for itself is mind-blowing. It can have ultimately tragic consequences. Quite a few men, having lost their jobs, often unexpectedly, have been so much in fear of the wrath of their wives and families if faced with the prospect of a reduced lifestyle that they have actually killed themselves. Others have continued to leave the house and return each day, as though still at work. . .

The above scenario is more likely to happen when the family concerned has been doing well, materially, by their own standards and the standards of those around them. The equally hard-working but less well paid, whose jobs may never have been regarded as particularly secure, are far more likely to receive sympathy and support from their peer group. The right-minded attitude of, 'I'll help him, I know he would help me', used to epitomize the solid decency to be found in the salt-of-the-earth members of the working class. Mercifully, this unfashionable response does survive.

In fact the first relatively well-off group should be pitied more. As they have been caught up in the lifestyle which has become so disproportionately important to them, they have been ignoring their own humanity, cheapening the real them. One of the effects of taking this attitude is that, ignoring the true values in life, the kindness, the caring, the loving people for themselves and not their appearances, they get caught up in an ever-increasing snowball of dissatisfaction.

* * *

The culture of 'must have' has always been there. People dashed out and bought their first black and white television sets so they could watch the coronation of Queen Elizabeth in 1953. These had small screens, were as deep as they were wide, and were very heavy. People crowded round them, and peered. There was another rush to the shops decades later, when everyone wanted to watch the wedding of Princess Anne to Captain Mark Phillips on the early colour TVs. Since then masses of different electrical items, microwaves, mobile phones, computers, I-pods have joined the list of things some people feel they must have if they are to be seen by others as successful. Up-dating computers etc. has become an obsession.

I think the young are particularly vulnerable. They have not become settled or established as people in their own eyes, and feel they must convince others of their blossoming success through a display of possessions. I started work when I was 18, and saved up for and bought my first old car, a 1956 Ford Popular – its twin can be seen in a motor museum – for £45. As soon as I could afford to I upgraded it to a Hillman Husky. . . then an Austin Cambridge. This progression mattered to me! Thank goodness I am now a bit wiser as well as older. I would see the possession of a status symbol car as a demonstration of my own insecurity – not to mention the fact that I would be displaying a selfish denial of the need to combat global warming.

Tragically many of the desperately insecure, while not having the money to buy the possessions they felt they must have, chose to run up massive debts through credit cards, and eventually found themselves in a terrible mess financially. If only their lives had been based on true, lasting values none of this would have happened. A culture in which people were valued for themselves, little kindnesses they could show to others, and where appearances were seen as irrelevant would have done away with the pressures fuelled by a materialistic society.

* * *

It will be a challenge for most, but there is the choice either to pander to the messages put across by the advertisers and the media or to get off the treadmill of materialism and make a stand for freedom – the freedom to apply individual judgement and decide on what really matters in life.

The fact that a need to identify with possessions is most keenly felt by the inadequate, and felt not at all by the truly successful, can be illustrated as described. The young criminals I worked with had a desperate need to own or be seen with BMW cars – that was their fashion of the day. By association they felt elevated in the presence of something they perceived as expensive. Few had legal driving licences, and none would have been able to get insurance cover. In conversation they implied that they would not have tolerated second-rate furniture in their homes – when I knew that in reality they lived in scruffy conditions. They felt the need to keep up a front.

By contrast I was once at a dinner party arranged at the home of a friend. His father had been invited – a man who had had a very distinguished career – who had a lengthy entry in Who's Who, and who lived in a massive house in a very expensive part of London. He had no need to make an impression. I silently applauded the fact that his pullover – which would have been a good one in its day – had splendid holes at the elbows. There sat a man wholly at ease with himself, and comfortable in his own skin.

However, one does not have to be outwardly successful to be at peace with oneself. In fact many successful people – fearful that their status might suddenly take a tumble – remain insecure and materially ambitious. Those with fewest possessions, by accident or design, may have the inner wisdom to know that owning things is no key to happiness in the deeper sense.

A simple life lived with the profound knowledge that it is the intangible and eternal that are the truly meaningful goals is worth a thousand of those spent indecently scrabbling after the latest meaningless gizmo. Only by acknowledging and responding to the needs of the humanity which lies deep within each one of us can we ever hope to achieve real peace and happiness.

* * *

The proof of this was demonstrated magnificently when a group of girls carried out an experiment. They were young, it took courage, and I admire them immensely! They agreed to give up wearing make-up, and they and a group of boys also stopped using computers, e-mails, mobile phones etc. which had all been integral parts of their lives.

This was indeed a challenge. However, they triumphed, and kept to their programme.

What were the results? The girls, sporting the lovely young faces nature had given them unobscured by powders and potions, found that their self-esteem rose. They came to understand that they were the people they truly were – not masks with no meaning. They had got genuine confidence, not dependent on artificial products.

And what about communication? The boys and girls make the discovery that without electronic link-ups they were forced (at first) to have much more personal contact with family and friends. It was not long before they realized the wonderful warmth, spontaneous responses, humour, and depth of understanding which blossomed through one-to-one contact in a way it never could in the stilted and impersonal communication offered by phones and computers.

With their new understanding these brilliant young people said that the experience had made them re-assess their values. Their deep humanity had always been with them, but a door had been opened which demonstrated indisputably that this was what really mattered. . . So much for the genuinely plastic, trivial, and posed woman trying to convince us that we cannot live without some perceived beauty product which we should rush out and buy because we are 'worth it'. How preposterous!

* * *

Sadly for many who have lost touch with the deep inner knowledge of themselves they have come to see their bodies in a completely material way, to receive up-dates and make-overs as though they were rooms in the house or the car standing in the drive.

Unhappily our bodies are in decline. We grow from babies into children from children to adults, and then embark – like it or not – on the road to physical deterioration. Well, that is one way of looking at it. Another is to see with relative awe and wonder the development of character which manifests in the faces of older people and which richly enhances our world.

There is definitely a place for cosmetic surgery, however. Children born with cleft palates and harelips deserve the finest treatment on offer. Those who have sustained horrific injuries in traffic or other accidents must be given all the help they can. What, then, of people with perfectly normal faces who pay huge sums of money to have them altered, and what of the surgeons who carry out this work rather than turning their attention to those with cruel disfigurements?

I would be lying if I did not have moments of utterly despising these people and their specialists. However, I know this reaction to be wrong. People who are so self-centred, prepared to spend fortunes on non-essential surgery when half the world is starving, are deserving of pity. These have truly lost their way.

No amount of fussing and flapping over saggy bits or wrinkles will have any effect on the real us. We are our inner selves, the selves of our own making, formed by our capacity to love those around us, help those who need it, offer words of comfort or support, and be honest, kind, and generous. The good but plain may not be wowed at the bus stop, but they are likely to have a wonderful circle of family and friends who would die for them, knowing, appreciating, and loving the qualities which really matter, and which are recognised and valued deeply.

* * *

What is perception? We cannot avoid having an initial reaction when we meet someone, very often based on physical characteristics. However, it is an awareness of the personality which takes over as we get to know them. It is the people they are which count – and their qualities which attract or repel us.

I had a friend who was Iranian. I appreciated his very good qualities, and was quite disturbed when, one day, he started ranting and raving because he said he had a darker skin that most Arabs, and looked more like a Pakistani. I blinked, looked again, and supposed that he was a shade darker than other Persians that I knew. But I was horrified at the outburst, and felt potentially offended at the thought that he might think his colour counted against him in my eyes.

While some allow themselves to be hurt by the way they look others have a capacity to be comfortable in their own skins, no matter what. There was a television programme about the possibility of surgeons carrying out face transplants. This event has since taken place, but at the time the medicos were looking for a candidate.

Their gaze fell on a woman who had had horrific burns to her face. Unavoidable, it was the first thing one noticed about her. Her nose had been reduced to two holes, and one marvelled that she could still eat and had retained her sight. However, as the programme progressed it was impossible to see the scars and what could have been regarded as the ugliness of this woman.

Along with unimaginable courage she radiated an inner peace, and quietly and confidently described the satisfaction she got from her good and simple life. Did she want her face removed and that of a corpse – possibly a beautiful corpse – put in its place? No, of course not. Life was fine as it was. There was a real chance if the operation went wrong she would die, and she certainly had no wish to lose the life which was meaningful to her.

Surely, if she was comfortable in her own skin, the rest of us should be content to remain as we are.

The Media – Celebrities And Soaps

The media may be encouraging antisocial behaviour by introducing it into soap operas. . . crimes are seen as more acceptable if carried out in soap operas or by celebrities. . . our society has become increasingly violent and all forms of crime should be discouraged. . . but some television programmes are positive and excellent. . . celebrities and their followers and their influence. . . what constitutes fame. . .? We must stand back and see celebs as the real people they are. . . accept what life has sent us. . . our quiet lives may bring us calm and satisfaction.

I sometimes wonder where we can go from here. Over the years I have seen a great relaxation in what is generally regarded as acceptable. We have now got to the point where television soaps – once featuring little more than fairly harmless tittle-tattle among the players and day-to-day events – now incorporate murder and rape into the story line. Those that watch regularly become involved with the characters – even though they know they are fictitious. My fear is that in bringing extremes of behaviour into people's homes in this way Jo Public will gradually absorb the idea that murder and rape are not so remote after all, and by being performed by people they feel they know may become more acceptable.

Indications show that the man in the street may be loathe to find a celebrity guilty – even if the alleged crime was vicious and violent – if he finds himself sitting on the jury. Judgement is swept aside so that a not guilty verdict is returned – flying in the face of evidence. This can only point to the fact that having a high profile and a lot of money raises the celebrity in the eyes of some members of the public to a status where he is above the law, and any crime is made acceptable because the person who committed it has a popular following.

Our society has become increasingly violent and threatening. Half a century ago no schoolchild would have considered carrying a knife to threaten violence and would have been ostracized had he done so. Gradually we have sunk into the situation where groups of emotionally damaged children form themselves into vindictive gangs and the leaders are the ones willing to inflict the greatest damage on harmless members of the public.

Anything which tends to encourage crime, or make it appear acceptable, should be condemned. We must not allow ourselves to become anaesthetized to the horrors in our world. We must understand that for everyone who is killed the potential of that life is lost, and family and friends are left grieving, and for those left injured their lives may never be the same again.

* * *

Where soaps are concerned there was one very hopeful sign. The scriptwriters of The Archers – Radio 4 – once started to incorporate the makings of affairs – completely out of character – for David and his wife Ruth. Regular listeners tended to switch off their sets seeing this move as stupid and unpleasant. Some who never bothered to listen said they thought they might – indicating the wish for squalid voyeurism which encourages the press and the rest of the media to pursue with avidity celebrities whose lives feature infidelity and addictions, outbursts of temper, or anything else over which the public can mock and crow.

On a very positive note, there are excellent television programmes which focus on the lives of animals in different parts of the world, and all sorts of interesting subjects. We are very lucky to have this knowledge at our fingertips, and so beautifully represented. Turning to nature can provide us with a wonderful therapy, whether we are walking in the woods or having a cup of tea in front of the telly. This is a real and meaningful way to escape from the problems in our lives.

It is very interesting that among the most popular programmes are the costume dramas often based on the novels of the writers of the past. These demonstrate the standard of values in place at the time – when good and bad were much more clearly defined. Almost always did the heroine win in the end, and any dishonest or scheming characters were seen to be punished and rejected.

I think this answers a deep-down wish that such a simple and right-minded attitude could remain an accepted part in our lives today.

* * *

The media is constantly at fever pitch over celebrities. Entertainment stars, footballers, and anyone deemed worthy of hitting the headlines is positively persecuted by photographers and journalists, whether they want to be or not. Often they start off loving the attention – it is good for their careers and preens their egos. Plenty end up sick of the publicity, and regretting their loss of privacy.

The public receive a blow-by-blow account of these people's lives, which are all too often of no significant importance. Any collapse into drugs or drink addiction is monitored almost by the minute. The discovery of an affair is big news – we are supposed to revel in it.

What is going on here? A tiny minority of the public will have crushes on these people, some knowing that their wishings and imaginings are pure fantasy, while others will live more and more in their world of make-believe. A handful will exhibit mental instability, and become stalkers.

Why are we supposed to be so interested in celebrities? Their fame and fortune will be seen by some to be the ideal way of escaping from mundane lives but, having no realistic chance of either coming their way they feel that, by knowing every detail of a celeb's life, they can identify with this person.

What makes theses people attractive to journalists and the masses? Little account is taken of their true qualities as people, whether they are good, kind, and generous. Once again it is wealth and the apparent power it gives which acts as a magnet. If hard work and genuine talent and good examples of solid family lives were on display the obsession with knowing every detail of the lives of others could be quite a positive form of escapism.

This is not the case. The more the celeb exhibits grossly selfish and anti-social trends the more coverage is given in the press and media generally. Mindless adulation of well-known names eats away consciously and subconsciously colouring the views of the members of the public. Gradually, and rather alarmingly, whatever these heroes do becomes acceptable. Cheating on wives and girlfriends or partners and boy-friends, spawning children on casual one night stands, throwing punches in pubs, driving under the influence of drink, sliding into alcohol or drug addiction, all these juicy aspects of their lives are revealed and chewed over by the media and the public who mop it up.

* * *

What of the realities of the lives of these celebrities? Many have come from relatively humble backgrounds and understandably are out of their depth and completely unable to cope with the huge amounts of money which suddenly come their way. They are expected to flash it about, following a lifestyle which was foreign to them and alien, but into which we expect them to slide without any problems. There will be advisors, agents, hangers-on, begging letters and unless the budding celeb is blessed with superhuman judgement he or she may well be conned and taken advantage of right from the start.

In reality the pressures will be immense. I suspect many new celebs scarcely realize this. Encouraged by those around them their standing in their own eyes blossoms like the mushroom-shaped cloud of a nuclear explosion, enveloping all with a me-and-my power protective blanket. Where is the celeb to go from there?

In the same way that young kids can enter a marriage believing that once the knot is tied all will be wonderful for ever, so the suddenly successful will find the future – in realistic terms – is infinitely more challenging. This is only the start. What lies ahead?

We have all seen the photographs and the snippets of film on the news. Our heroes – deliciously fallen – stagger out of night clubs drunk or drugged, are caught – all credit to them – entering or exiting rehabilitation clinics, being led away in handcuffs or approaching or leaving a court as a result of facing charges of violent behaviour, drug-related offences, or trying to avoid paying income tax. Sometimes it is not the celeb but friends who may well have been paid handsomely for revealing facts – possibly accurate, possibly not – about intimate details of the private life of the victim, which appear in the media.

* * *

So – is this the 'happiness' we crave? Plodding away at our mundane, but much more protected, lives would we thrive any better if extreme fame and fortune came our way? Almost certainly not. Instead of revelling in the misfortunes – for misfortunes they are – of these people who regularly hit the headlines we should stand back and see them for what they are, ordinary, not superhuman, vulnerable not indestructible, and invited to experience the happiness of their lives only at one, trivial level.

These people have, at their core, the same need to express their humanity as the rest of us. They need times of peace to connect up with their inner selves, respond by giving and receiving love at a constant and meaningful level. A man who has been married or in a stable partnership for years is much more likely to be able to achieve this. Each night he lies by the same woman. They trust each other, and share the feelings of protection and concern over their children. Life is predictable, solid, and real. This is where true contentment lies – the reward for leading life as a thoroughly good, kind, decent person.

Some celebs have had good marriages. Cilla Black is a shining example of this. It is possible, though, that as she pursued her career her children felt they would have liked her to spend more time with them. But there was a lot of genuine love in that family, for which they are to be congratulated.

* * *

If we are to heal society we must again stand back, accept the celebrities for what they are, just people like ourselves with the same needs. We should avoid being judgemental, understanding that the paths their lives have taken will have proved unbelievably challenging. Without jealousy we must also learn to be content with whatever life has sent us. Being bitter because we have fewer material possessions is harmful to ourselves and solves nothing.

Standing back still further we could feel glad if we have not been tempted to let our own lives sink into the morass of greed, selfishness, egotism, and arrogance which is so often and proudly exhibited by celebrities, and which is splashed all over the pages of the newspapers or recorded on the television.

The saying that 'All publicity is good publicity' may be true. But what is good for publicity may well be tragically destructive for the celeb whose antics have been described. Their addictions may indicate a desperate need to escape, and we can ponder the fact that quite a few commit suicide, or die an early death.

Some remind me of a firework. They rise into the air, explode into a brilliant shower of stars, and then fall to earth and are quickly forgotten.

AMBITION, COMPETITION, AND SUCCESS

What is true success. . . ? What is success as the world sees it. . . ?
How do we cope if our possessions and status are endangered. . . ?
Some seek to bask in reflected glory. What is the true meaning of
reward. . . ? The concept of ownership.

I would define true success as someone achieving a state of
mind which is calm and peaceful. This will have been the
result of expressing innate humanity through showing love
and concern to other human beings.

There will be nothing tangible about this – no outer
manifestation of wealth or even beauty – though such people
often exude an indefinable quality which others find attracts
them very strongly.

Our society, as it is arranged, cares little for such things.
How is a child doing at school? Would there ever be the reply
that the little person was showing sensitivity towards those
who were unhappy in his class, being kind to anyone
handicapped or not very bright – the target of criticism? No,
the response would be about academic or some other
achievement.

* * *

Competition, ambition, and success are concepts usually
applied to easily observable phenomena – the results of tests or
exams, a desire to get promotion, buying flash new cars, being
seen to have made a lot of money, doing better than other
people. Doing better? What do we mean by that? Scrambling
after status and material gain takes no account of what is going
on inside the people who get caught up in this race.

Every now and again we get an insight into how pre-posterous the state of mind can become. A banker discovered that he would no longer get his £3,000,000 bonus so he killed himself. Already loaded down with possessions which would not be denied him, it was beyond him to accept how unbelievably well favoured he still was compared with other people. But that is a false statement. He was not well-favoured. He had lost his true standard of values and had become dependent on a lifestyle full of emptiness. He had turned his back on the humanity which should have been driving him, and he feared that his substitute was to be taken from him. In fact he should have been pitied, not mocked which was many people's – quite understandable – response.

* * *

It would be ridiculous to pretend that life is not competitive, and it would be unrealistic to think otherwise. In a perfect world we would compete only with ourselves, doing the best we could and feeling happily satisfied with our effort. But we are not destined to escape so lightly.

We need to have our basic needs met, and most of us want a lot more that that – often more for our families than for ourselves. We are coerced into the rat race, like it or not. However, while we go through the motions of conforming to what we may recognise as a deeply flawed pattern, we can at least retain an independence of mind. We do what we have to, but we know that there is much more to life than that. If redundancy or some other disaster strikes we know that our humanity is untouched. We are still the kind, honourable, and good people that we always were. This deep and right-minded self-belief will help us through terrible situations.

Some opt out of making effort themselves by pinning their ambitions on another person. Parents – who have often achieved little – make their child's or children's lives miserable by wanting to live their own lives through them, hoping for power and glory. These children are not allowed to fail. They must bring honour to their parents, arouse praise – and, even better, envy – from other parents, and generally spite those around them by out-doing them. Nasty. Very nasty. But far from unknown. There are also wives who bully their husbands into improving their status, and husbands who value their wives only as attractive decorations to arouse the jealousy of other men with more homely spouses.

We need not get caught up in this syndrome. But we should spare a thought for the probably obnoxious and precocious brats or the henpecked husbands. They are in most unenviable positions, and are the victims.

* * *

What do we mean by 'reward'? It has come to mean little more than material remuneration in many cases. If reward – and logically it should – means happiness then we are barking up the wrong tree by equating money or possessions with happiness. Certainly it is true that genuine poverty will result in unhappiness. We all have basic and essential needs which must be met and if they are not then we will suffer. But there is a world of difference between this, and the spoilt child 'unhappiness' caused by being unable to indulge oneself with more and more unnecessary luxuries.

Happiness does not manifest – at least certainly not in any lasting form – through the material. It is a state of mind. Contentment is one of the greatest gifts we can have. Some families feel the need to constantly up-grade their homes, their cars, their clothes, their holidays. . . and in reality they are simply running away from themselves, from their own states of mind. A restless, dissatisfied mind demands distractions.

People with contented minds can settle in the same home for years, hang on to a car until it becomes unreliable, and do not – in spite of apparently lowly circumstances – perceive themselves as to be judged by their external trappings. No, they have a much more peaceful attitude, and know their value as human beings is a much deeper thing.

* * *

When I worked with young criminals appearance was desperately important to them. This really was tragic, as many were poor, and no-hopers. Only by crime, and flashing the proceeds of it, could they envisage raising their status. The idea that value lay in the expression of their own innate humanity would never have occurred to them. This was a great shame, as many of them did have, at the core, many good qualities. They could love their family, unexpectedly respond by wanting to help someone in distress, care for rescued animals. They could not credit themselves with the true values that they had.

These people – and many others much better placed in society – have got caught up in the material and intangible success and failure syndrome. This excludes the acknowledgement of much deeper and more profound aspects of life – the aspects of which the topsy-turvy world of possessions and position takes no account.

* * *

Ambition, competition, and success are like a snowball which gathers momentum. Driven by the desire to reach the top – whatever the man-invented and meaningless top may be – a new top has to be found if the original one is reached. The struggle towards it has become the driving force in life, and appears to be essential for survival. This mad struggle is in complete contrast to the peace and calm achieved by those whose aim is to develop a closer link to their own humanity.

We must not let ourselves get caught up in the rat race, but be prepared to accept our apparently humbler positions – so much richer in the true human qualities of life.

Consider the experience of a child from an ordinary family with a caring father. Daddy takes him off to football, helps him fly his kite, makes him things, shows him how he can make things, and the boy is thoroughly involved with a man who loves him and whom he adores in return. They spend many hours together.

By contrast another father – a chequebook Daddy – has almost no contact with his son. Lavish clothing will be bought, boarding school fees paid, and the environment, house and car exude wealth. But where is the empathy, the comfortable, unspoken understanding between them? On the surface there may appear to be no need for such things – but underneath there is a great chasm, a void with nothing to fill it.

Is the child from a wealthy background destined to do well? I have seen students leave very expensive schools having achieved little – they have suffered from parental neglect of a different kind. They have an additional disadvantage. Cocooned in an expensive environment they are ill equipped to face the harsh realities of the world if and when they need to. Again, as so often, potential is lost.

POLITICAL CORRECTNESS

*Political correctness stands between us and necessary serious debate. . .
racial issues. . . the benefits system. . . seeing obesity as an illness. . .
failing to accept that not all students are academic. . . conversely failing
to value those in blue-collar jobs. . . while the gay community can get
away with exhibitionism more easily than a heterosexual. Reasoned
discussion on all matters – no matter how inflammatory – must be
allowed and encouraged if those who feel aggrieved are to be pacified.
Political correctness can protect the vulnerable. . . but those who are at
fault should not be able to shelter behind it.*

Political correctness is often a very damaging influence in our
lives – it stifles debate on many issues which trouble us, and
which need to be addressed. The longer we delay getting to
the roots of problems the worse they become, and the harder
to remedy. A lot of really important matters are affected.

Take the very vexed subject of racial issues. In every nation
be it England, Nigeria, Germany, Pakistan, France, America,
or Poland there are good, bad, and average people. It may be
a popular conception that the nationals of individual
countries have particular characteristics which we do or do
not like. If someone is called a 'Paki' this is usually regarded
as an insult. Why? There are so many kind, good, generous
Pakistanis who make wonderful neighbours and this should
be acknowledged. I think we tackle this problem from the
wrong direction. Instead of living with the image of an
undesirable Pakistani we should be educated to see the virtues
of so many of that race, so the term could not be seen as an
insult.

More muddled thinking goes on around our perception of
foreigners. They come to our shores to do us out of our jobs –
often low-paid ones – or they come and scrounge off our
benefits system, National Health Service etc. In fact the

problem is not these people's nationality or where they come from – it is the sort of people they are. There are plenty of English people who abuse the system of state handouts subsidised by the hard-working section of the populous, and these are also the ones who tend to waste the time of accident and emergency departments in the hospitals and pester their doctors unnecessarily.

The government – which can be far too soft in dealing with the lazy malingerers who were born here – is at fault in not weeding out foreigners with these characteristics to stop them from coming to our shores. They cannot expect to be welcome.

So far as immigrants taking low-paid jobs are concerned one is tempted to say, for the British who shunned such jobs in the good times when they could earn well but who, out of work, found they needed to accept any position they could find, that it was a bit of an own goal.

Political correctness filtered down the benefits system so that it was seen as wrong that those who were not pulling their weight might have to accept a lower standard of living. This applied much less to single people than it did to families – more people, more votes – so that women, with or without partners, do handsomely by just producing children they have no intention of supporting financially. If there is a long-term partner he is in clover, work being an unattractive option while he can laze around at home surrounded by children, with the odd trip to the pub to see his mates.

No one would want to see the children hungry, but the present system encourages sponging and idleness. If food and clothing vouchers are seen as infringing the rights of these people to choose how our money is spent – tough. If taxpayers' funds were allocated to specific domestic outgoings rather that being dished out as hefty sums of cash the option of remaining as a parasite would appear much less attractive.

But political correctness backed up by the human rights concept, which has become so much more ridiculous since we entered the European Union, deters any UK government from having the guts to tackle the matter – and this applies to many others.

* * *

Take for example the problem of obesity. Very few people have genuine glandular defects. Most people, particularly the young, are fat because they over eat and under exercise. But the grossly overweight regard themselves as ill, and expect medical treatment at the taxpayers' expense. One woman wanted a free operation but, finding she was not quite fat enough to qualify, went on a binge-eating spree. It is disgusting that people are not told to take responsibility for themselves, as they should.

* * *

Many alcoholics and gamblers have sorted themselves out by joining A.A. or Gamblers Anonymous. We already have Weight Watchers and possibly a similar group – but for the grossly obese – could be set up. Let the problem be acknowledged and tackled by forming groups of fellow-sufferers who could establish friendships and support each other in their battle to eat less and become more physically active.

* * *

Yet another, and to my mind huge, problem has arisen because we believe it wrong to make distinctions between people. This should not imply 'criticism' but as simply acknowledging that we are all individuals, and are not all the same.

Everyone is supposed to be clever enough to go to university, at least if they go to good schools and have good backgrounds. To accept less than a degree course is seen as inferior. The result is that school examination standards have been dummed down so that more and more people can enter more and more – often completely useless – degree courses.

In kidding ourselves that these students are all academic we do them a terrible disservice. They are unlikely to find the rewarding jobs they had envisaged and, horror or horrors, they may have to accept employment in posts they had been brought up to think of as demeaning.

This is a perfect example of political correctness shooting itself in the foot and scoring an own goal. While there was the heavily implied criticism that anything less than a university education and a clean, white-collar job was unacceptable, the attitude taken to jobs perceived to be lower in the social pecking order received a snooty disregard.

Electricians, builders, plumbers, street cleaners, window cleaners – all these are people the country depends upon. Political correctness has demonstrated prejudice by never crediting these often very skilled individuals with their true roles in our lives. If political correctness had any meaningful purpose it would sing the praises of, and invite us to respect, people who work hard at often not very well-paid jobs.

* * *

When ill-thought through political correctness – often manifesting in government decisions and laws we do not like – results in what we see as the wrong people having an unfair advantage we have to, once again, stand back. The situation is out of our hands. Getting bitter and jealous damages ourselves and does nothing to remedy the situation. Try hard to see any good you can in the 'winners' who may be, for instance, playing the system by sending our money abroad, but may, in their own eyes, simply be helping their families overseas.

* * *

Gay rights is another topic about which political correctness has gone overboard.

This book is about us expressing our humanity – our love for each other. This has nothing to do with sexual proclivity. If there is good caring love it matters not, if sexual and all parties are happy with the arrangement, whether it is between men and women, men and men, or women and women. It is how we all treat each other that counts.

Cheating when in a relationship is equally damaging and hurtful no matter what the genders of the partners. What does matter is that we are mindful of the effects of our behaviour – whether we will hurt those who are close to us.

There are promiscuous people in all groups and if they distress others they should expect to receive criticism. There is a tendency for some to think that relationships between men are likely to involve less commitment, partly because there is no danger of a child being conceived. While this may be fine for some, it will be devastating for others – just as infidelity can destroy the happiness of an innocent husband or wife.

I do not think nature intended sex to be the subject of great displays. The act of starting a new and precious life is usually carried out in the private intimacy of the home – a home which will welcome the little baby.

Sure, woman like to dress up and men like to look smart if they are going for a night out which is a bit of an occasion, but on the whole they feel no need to go as raw sex symbols. Anyone who really overdoes it may be regarded as flashy, ridiculous or loose and not necessarily desirable – even if eye-catching.

Carried to an extreme certain types of clothing border on – or even cross the line into – exhibitionism. Brilliant, if someone wants to go wild in his or her own home, and invite selected friends along. But must we have overt displays in the streets? Perfectly normal children and the parents who are trying to bring them up well have to use the same streets, and is it right that they should be subjected to this?

Obviously there are well-publicised events where the gay community let their hair down, and it is up to those out of sympathy with the cause to keep away, but on a day-to-day basis public displays of extreme clothing or behaviour are distasteful. There is nothing anti-gay about this. A woman who spent her time doing ordinary chores, shopping, etc., dressed as an over-the-top prostitute, or a bloke for ever wearing exaggeratedly tight trousers so no-one could avoid noticing his prick would be equally offensive, and probably openly recognized as such.

Most people of every persuasion have friends of all sexual proclivities. Many women find that gay men make the most wonderful friends – sympathetic and dependable. I am completely heterosexual but, in spite of the fact my mother sexually abused me when I was a child, I greatly value kind lesbian friends – who would never dream of trying to involve me in their activities.

We are all people. We all need to give and receive love, and the greater the number and diversity of people with whom we can share this the better our lives will be. Making ourselves exclusive in any way is counter productive. Most of us have to adapt in some ways, with some people, to be acceptable. Let us be sensitive to the needs of others so that we can all richly enjoy each other's company as our humanity wishes us to.

* * *

Of course, the up-side of political correctness is that fewer hurtful remarks will be made to further damage the vulnerable. However, is politely ignoring any problem going to solve it? Any wound has to be lanced and the poison drained away – smothering it with a coating of face powder will solve nothing and tend to make it worse.

Discussion of a person's or society's problems should be encouraged. If any subject is treated sensitively and with compassion there is a real chance that a solution, or at least a partial solution, will be found.

The very act of having an open debate can be cathartic.

Many have strong opinions on topics which – because of political correctness – they will be condemned for bringing to the surface. These festering sores will be partly healed by the very fact they have been allowed to be aired, and a reasoned discussion has been allowed to take place.

Those who feel embittered because, for instance, they believe that foreigners have invaded their area and been allotted scarce housing facilities, should have every opportunity to voice their concerns and opinions. Dialogue between them and the invaders is far more likely to achieve harmony in the community than by gagging the aggrieved party.

However when high temperatures run with such matters the aim should be to achieve a calm and reasoned discussion with all the venom taken out. If the angry are given the opportunity to have their views heard and taken seriously they will feel valued. It is what they perceive as their impotence in these situations which inflames matters. We should accept that those who appear to be hostile and vindictive – albeit with a reasoned cause – have true humanity at their hearts, and we should acknowledge this and value them, making allowances for their circumstances if necessary.

Equally, if someone is greedy and playing the system unfairly this should be openly acknowledged. An irresponsible Englishwoman who banged out a string of children from the age of fifteen in order to get a house of her own, or a family who happened to be coloured and were also playing the system, should definitely not be immune from criticism.

Rights And Freedoms

Freedom – a splendid concept. . . but can expressing that freedom damage others. . . ? on the international stage should one country have the freedom to damage another. . . ? or its own nationals. . . ? terrible damage has been done to some countries by others expressing what they want to see as their 'right'. . . and the freedom as expressed by the actions of individuals can also have consequences on a personal level. . . we must understand that others have rights and freedoms as well as ourselves.

Freedom – a magnificent concept and something we should all have as a right. This is easily said, but more complex to define. In order for freedom to be acceptable one immediately has to start imposing limits. Freedom for one person must not be dependent on or involve the restriction of another. One's freedom to express one's dislike of another can hardly be acceptable if it involves punching or stabbing him. But how does this apply to countries?

I was very uneasy when I saw George Bush, the then President of America, greeted as 'the leader of the free world'. What 'world'? Were they referring to America, or the West? Did they mean that America is 'free'? But the term is still used today. By 'free' do they mean that all men are equal, having equal rights and equal opportunities? If they think this they are sadly deluded. In the richest country on earth there are plenty of ethnic factions who feel disadvantaged, plenty of extremely poor people who over the years have been ignored or ridden over roughshod by the more wealthy, plenty who have not been treated when they were sick as they could not meet the bills.

The term free world – what does that mean? Over the years America has imposed – or tried to impose – its regime over countries that want none of this interference, and even less wanted to see their people slaughtered during military invasions. But because of the power their wealth has given America – or to be accurate the top strata of the country – they arrogantly assume they have the right to re-organize the world the way they want it, completely ignoring the tragic destruction of people they have invented as enemies, Koreans, Vietnamese, Iraqis. . .

America and every other powerful, bullying nation would have to change its mindset to allow freedom to those they wish to control. China – for many years a country about which the inner workings were a mystery to the rest of the world – also displays the control freak mentality. The Chinese are ruthless with their own people to a degree which is mind-blowing to most of us in the west. Those whose homes stood in the path of the Olympic village were evicted, and their homelessness ignored. Hearing that visiting countries did not like to see litter on the streets there were horrific pictures of cats being rounded up and slaughtered in their masses, to tidy the place up.

Cruel to animals and cruel to people. Couples were only allowed to have one child each. An unwanted daughter may well have been left dead and disowned in the street. Students and other demonstrators were slaughtered on Tienanmen Square. The anniversary of this atrocious massacre was not acknowledged by the authorities in 2009.

The English have nothing to be proud of. In the horribly mistaken belief that their sort of freedom gave them the right to govern India their way, they were responsible for the Amritsar Massacre, where, in 1919, the British opened fire on an unarmed crowd killing 380 and injuring 1,200.

The 'freedom' of nations is a false concept, I think. The leaders of nations have never been humble – with the probable exception of Mahatma Ghandi. Arrogantly, they want to have everything their way. The Suez crisis in the 1950s saw the English government apparently believing they had a right to own the Suez Canal in all but name, when in fact that strip of waterway never had and never would belong to them, and they had been extremely lucky to have had the use of it for so long.

Blair was reported to have been obsessed with contemplating his 'place in history'. The result was, along with Bush, he ordered the invasion of Iraq on a completely false pretext. In doing so, not only did he deny the freedom of life to thousands or Iraqis, injuring many more, and leaving them without homes, jobs, water, and electricity, but he failed to tackle the grave problems at home, crime, immigration, education, public finance – which blew up so dramatically after he had escaped from office. He had been given the freedom to do this.

It can be noted that two of the most decent and honourable members of his party – foreign secretary Robin Cooke and Mo Molem – who both opposed his plan to invade Iraq were treated shabbily. They both died, and he attended neither funeral. They were too good for him. The only freedom these morally superior souls had been able to exercise was to resign. This further stifled the freedom of the electorate opposed to the war to be represented by those who shared their views.

* * *

The abuse of freedom on an international scale has devastating consequences. The abuse of freedom on a one-to-one basis can be catastrophic, too, for those involved.

The freedom of an open road and a fast car – the thrill of speed – is great provided the enjoyment is taken responsibly. If there is a possibility of a blind bend, brow of a hill, or an approaching motorist freedom must give way to awareness of possible danger. Here freedom must be controlled fun, not an opportunity for the spillage of blood.

The office party scenario – freedom from the wife and a bit tipsy from the wine – off the leash! – a grope in the stationery cupboard – always fancied that little blond bit – and now she's seeing me as a one-night stand. Grab that freedom while I've got it. . . Later, unfortunately, I discover she did not want a one-night stand. She's become a bloody nuisance. Yes, I did fancy her – but I didn't plan to ditch the wife and kids for heaven's sake. . . Oh, bloody hell, the wife's found out. I really didn't mean this. . . Jeez. . . What a mess. I slink home to my saddened wife. . . no, I really didn't mean this. . .

* * *

The freedom to carry a knife – albeit illegally – I'm Jack the lad. Look at me as I sink the pints and chasers. Never mind the law, everyone carries knives. Yes, I might have had one too many, but I'm not stopping now. It's Saturday night and I do what I like. Some dick-head pushes ahead of me at the bar – I'm not taking that. I shove him and he shoves back. We fight. I wield the knife. There is confusion. It all goes a bit foggy, and I find myself being pulled about by policemen. . .

Few people set out with bad intentions. Restrictions in their lives often mean they are too easily tempted to freak out. Too little awareness of one's own responsibility can be disastrous, for oneself and others. Personal freedom cannot give the right to risk damaging others. Laws – like the banning of knives – must be obeyed. If tempted, think before you act and accept that you cannot ignore the effect you may have on others. They have their rights and freedoms, too. Respect them.

PART FOUR

WHAT WE SEE AROUND US

THE POLICE AND
THE JUSTICE SYSTEM

The terrible problem of child criminals. . . the rudderless under 25s and their bleak future. . . how do the police handle crime. . . ? but they get little encouragement even if they do their job well. . . likely offenders have been given a lot of freedom. . . are sentences fair. . . ? is it reasonable that public money is used so that criminals can exercise possible human rights claims. . . ? all too often it appears that fraud pays.

Our children are being encouraged to grow up fast. One reason for this is that some parents – rather that wallowing in their offsprings' infanthood – hope to see them as budding adults as soon as possible.

Alarmingly, there are growing numbers of junior criminals some of whom are guilty of very serious crimes indeed. Their extreme youth poses the problem of what to do with them, how to view them, how to treat them.

The problem is not new. When I was on the press bench of a local magistrates court in the 1960s I saw a boy put into care just after his eighth birthday. Had he been an adult he would already have spent years in goal for offences of dishonesty. He was a very successful cat burglar. Many of his exploits – climbing drainpipes, scaling roofs – meant that he put himself in danger. His parents feared to lock him in his bedroom – he would probably have climbed through the first-floor window.

The father, sitting behind him, was in tears. He and his wife really had tried, he said. The boy was completely unmoved. It was a very chilling moment. He fixed each member of the bench, and myself, with an icy stare. It was a shock. Seen from the back he had lovely dark wavy hair – from the front there were those impenetrable eyes.

In Britain today there are a number of very discreetly positioned secure units for the worst of theses young offenders, whose crimes can include murder, rape – committed, it would appear as soon as it was physically possible – and sadistically violent crimes.

I have no idea how you can heal these situations. Certainly many of the children had terrible home backgrounds. The family of one pair of brothers were alleged to have encouraged them to fight each other, almost as though they had been substitutes for illegal dog fighting. Love and care and sympathy, discipline and guidance – if these do not work, nothing will. But to try to begin to understand these children's mindsets, where their thoughts and actions come from, is unbelievably daunting.

* * *

In August 2009 there were reports that there were over 900,000 young and men and women, under 25 years of age, who were not in work or any kind of education or training. Another statistic showed that during the next ten years one in six would be expected to have died, usually from alcohol or drug abuse, although suicide and violence also featured in figures which had been compiled following earlier research. This is a tragic situation and reflects the extreme problems in society.

* * *

For those who are the victims of crime, rather than the perpetrators, is there confidence in the way the police handle matters or that, if brought to justice, criminals will be given appropriate punishments?

The police feel they have inadequate funding although huge sums have been poured into the system. Probably the rise in crime, much of which appears to go unrecorded, explains this.

I personally know of, and have read of more, cases where the police have received 999 calls from people being threatened or burgled at the time they have rung, and the police have taken between half an hour and four hours to respond. In each case an offender or offenders could have been caught red-handed, but all got away.

The police, however, have their own problems. They may move heaven and earth to nail an offender, and then see the Crown Prosecution Service refuse to take action.

In one instance a driver, already disqualified and well known to the police, was seen to hit a pedestrian – who nearly died – before racing away. A great deal of police work went into making what most of us would have seen as a watertight case, including prints on the car's dashboard, smashed so the criminal could over-ride the ignition. The CPS refused to act, inexplicably saying there was not enough evidence.

Government guidelines – prompted by the fact that more prisons had not been built when they should have been – encouraged offenders to be allowed bail or let out of goal early. Others who should have been detained were given non-custodial sentences. One set of figures showed that one in seven murders were committed by people who were on probation.

Between 1984 and 1998 a total of 1,600 were on the run from prison. These included 19 murderers and 26 sex offenders. It is not unreasonable to assume that they will have committed many more crimes during their ill-gotten freedom.

When criminals are found guilty their sentences must often be a big disappointment to the police, although their policy of dealing with some probable rapists, and those guilty of violent crimes being given a caution rather than being brought before the courts, beggars belief.

* * *

Life is cheap. A drunken driver who had a crash left his girl friend to die in the burning car, although he retrieved her mobile phone, got six years. While he was out on bail awaiting the trial he had been disqualified from driving for failing to provide a sample.

A drug-abusing man killed his girl friend's two-year-old son. He also got six years. We all know that the actual term served would be much shorter. . .

. . . A vulnerable pensioner was conned out of £370,000 by a gang who did £5,000 worth of work on a house worth £180,00. Initially given five years and eight months the sentence was cut to three years on an appeal by the rogue trader. . .

* * *

If public money is saved by keeping people out of prison it can be lavished on those within. It was expected that £5,000 of legal aid would be granted to a man who had raped and strangled a seven-year-old child, so that he could win the right to vote in elections while in prison.

A prisoner serving a sentence for killing three boys was originally awarded £66,400 damages as the Home Office had failed to provide dental work to cure toothache – this had included £250 for every week of his alleged suffering. A Home office appeal failed but the award was cut to £44,500.

A rapist – an immigrant – regarded as a threat to the public was handcuffed when taken to hospital for treatment. He claimed his human rights were breached. The British taxpayer shelled out £20,000 so that the immigrant could have legal aid to pursue his case, and when he died his daughter was allowed to continue to pursue damages, costing the taxpayer many thousands of pounds more.

* * *

I have noted countless cases where large sums - £30-£40,000 is not uncommon – have been obtained by benefit cheats or other means of fraud. Almost never is there the condition that the money should be repaid. One woman escaped prison claiming her daughter would have to be cared for by her grandmother abroad if she was sent down.

But prison appears to be a relatively rare outcome in any case. One woman was given a 12-month sentence but it was suspended for a year. She had stolen £45,000 in false benefit claims, but had only to pay £5,600 in prosecution costs, and do some community work. Message – fraud pays.

While the official line appears to be that people should be allowed to keep their ill-gotten gains there is little deterrent so far as the potentially dishonest are concerned.

* * *

We – the right-minded who couldn't live with ourselves if we behaved in this way – will and must stick to our guns. While officialdom appears to take a soft and indulgent line when dealing with those who steal from the rest of us, or do worse, we must simply help others, particularly the up-and-coming generation, to remain good and honest, and not to see these injustices as a temptation.

CRIMINALS

If you are a criminal please read on. . . I may like you and I know that there is a lot of good in you – let yourself show it. . . criminals – try not to hate them blindly. . . take their backgrounds into account and recognise how damaged they are. . . try to find a point of contact if possible. . . acknowledge their good points. . . but above all the innocent must be protected from them. . . some prisoners love to be there while others kill themselves. . . though I believe this is probably as a result of inner despair and not the prison conditions. . . I offer a suggestion of how some might be able to turn their lives around.

If you are a criminal do not feel excluded or attacked by this book. When I worked with criminals I got very fond of some of them who had many good qualities. Only a few – with bad records of violence and very hot tempers, a potentially explosive combination – presented big challenges.

Some people hate criminals. A bag may have been snatched or a house invaded and trashed by burglars and the victims may say quite openly that they could kill those responsible.

Hating does no good. It is destructive to ourselves and does not affect the object of our loathing. Blind hatred is usually an immediate response rather than a considered one. If we are to heal ourselves – let alone society – we must try to avoid this sort of thing.

One of the best ways for a healing to take place between the criminal and the victim can be for them to meet. This may not always be successful, but it is far from unknown for the criminal, suddenly confronted with another, suffering human being, to feel remorse, while the victim may meet a very disadvantaged kid and be able to see that ignorance and stupidity, rather than downright wickedness, might have been behind the crime.

What is in fact happening here, if the approach is helpful, is that all concerned are confronted by the others' humanity. The awareness of this, conscious or unconscious, shows a common bond which draws people together with a mutual sympathy rather than pushing them apart.

* * *

Natural reactions make us what we are. If we are hurt we show it, whether the damage is mental or physical. This is a part of being human. Is it possible to detect, even in hardened criminals, a hopeful sign – a spontaneous smile, a hint of affection?

If there is anything which might indicate that there can be a point of contact we must go for it. While incapable of establishing friendships with good people – and they would be ill-advised to place too much trust in their drug-dealing buddies – some have a genuine love for their dogs. Doggie talk might just offer a chink in the door. There was a case of a man in prison who had been guilty of a particularly vile murder. When he was told his dog had died he broke down and wept. The chances are that he had felt himself able to share love with a dog because – unlike the people in his life – he knew it would not hurt him.

Of course the murder he committed was terrible, but if people had treated him badly as he grew up he placed no value on them or their lives, expected the worst from them, and would be able to dispatch them with relative ease. I am not excusing, but showing how someone's history may explain how he had slipped into a life of destruction.

The young criminals I worked with were not hardened cases. Many of them, however, had sad and inadequate backgrounds. With most it was not difficult to form a good working relationship. There was a basic formula which worked quite well. Very conscious of their poor educational backgrounds I let if be known that I did not see them as stupid or ignorant. Most were not at all stupid – they had just lacked the opportunity and encouragement to take studies seriously.

Another insight into their lives came when I heard them discussing their cooking skills – hardly enhancing the macho image they generally wanted to portray. The 'I can make a good pasta' indicated that if the youngster wanted a decent meal he had to cook it himself. There was no mother prepared to put a good dish of steaming food in front of him, any more than she was willing or able to give support in any other way.

* * *

Whatever their apparent bravado almost all were actually very vulnerable and sensitive. I remember driving a group of them out to a new job – they did not know where they were going. In the mirror I saw two brothers – undersized through generations of poor dietary habits and general deprivation – perched on the edge of their seats. Their expressions were full of anxiety and they reminded me of a pair of terrified woodland mice. In fact, logic would have told them that they had no cause for concern. Rules and regulations ensured they would be perfectly safe wherever they were going, and they would be taken back to base on time.

Keeping a relaxed atmosphere was essential. There was a tendency for them either to be tense or making a rather over-done show of being at ease. Once our relationship was established and we were comfortable with each other things worked well. Over tea or coffee it was good to have a chat – possibly about plans any of them had, or general matters. A sense of humour helped. If you could actually get them to laugh or give way to a smile – they tended to want to scowl as much as possible – you had done rather well.

Once we were saying how long the kettle was taking to boil, and I told them how my kettle at home had a faulty thermostat and kept switching itself on and off, making little wittering sounds to itself as it did so. My imitation of the sound caught them unawares, and they forgot themselves, and found it funny.

Not reacting was another trick. Once we were working in a building which had a little fenced-in back garden. We drifted out and I realized, just too late, that they had planned to nip back inside and lock the door behind me. The fence was not very high and there was a store, out of sight, which was half its height and onto which I could climb. I was quickly on the other side, and I slowly and nonchalantly went through the front door and drifted back into the room where they sitting without showing any reaction at all. They nearly jumped out of their skins!

* * *

These, as I have said, were not hardened cases. They were young, and there was some hope left. I remember seeing one of the lads in town. He spotted one of his mates and went over to him. There was such an obvious show of spontaneous affection that I knew there was, indeed, much good in these people. But they do need opportunities. Training for skilled manual jobs would be ideal for many of them. Society would do well to make this sort of investment – for its own sake, as well as for theirs.

Do not think I am in favour of being soft on crime – I am not. Anything which sends out the message that you can 'get away with it' is completely counter-productive. I would also go for zero tolerance, then everyone knows exactly where he or she stands.

Whatever the hard-luck stories of the criminals priority must be given to protecting the public. If this means building a hundred more prisons, so be it. We cannot heal society by allowing people to repeat their crimes over and over again.

* * *

How is prison viewed by some of the inmates? A bunch of young female offenders liked life on the inside. It compared favourably with what awaited them outside – homelessness or hostels, vulnerability, and insecurity. They loved the food and the friends they made. So much for their 'other' lives. I felt it said it all.

At the other end of the scale I would suggest – and I did know one lad who killed himself – that it is not the prisons themselves that reduce people to suicide. It is the acknowledgement that, having committed oneself to a life of crime, the future is just too black to face. If these tragic cases felt they had meaningful futures I do not think that a few nights in a prison cell would reduce them to despair. Some, I think, have taken what they see as a rational look at what lies ahead, and have decided to quit. Sadly, one is forced to respect that decision.

I was furious to see a tabloid sneering at a young murderer because his mother was a prostitute earning money to feed her drug addiction. Far from being seen – as it was presented – as a further black mark against the youth it should have invited speculation about the home from hell he had probably experienced as he grew up.

This is a typical illustration of how the media – in the same way that they may adulate the famous and wealthy – love to vilify in any way possible those who have fallen from grace.

On being convicted many criminals will find the history of their lives – exclusions from schools, battles with the neighbours, traumas with common-law step-parents – splashed all over the papers. I would applaud this if the facts were presented as offering an explanation of how they became the sort of people who could harm their fellow men with such impunity. Just sometimes a newspaper will do this. Excellent!

All babies are born to be loved and to love. A small child who receives no love, or whose love is repelled, soon learns to cut off from the world. He kills the emotions which caused him so much pain. In self-defence he is separating himself from his humanity.

* * *

The capacity for forgiveness in the hearts of those who live close to their own humanity can be truly awesome.

During the Omagh bombing of 1998 a father held his daughter's hand as they both lay trapped. They shared, for the last time, the feelings of love for each other, as her life ebbed away. He did not respond to her death with hatred or bitterness. His lovely girl, a nurse, had been lost forever and he just felt deep sorrow and regret.

If a man can react in this way under those circumstances the rest of us should try not to react too violently if we become the victims of relatively minor crimes where a few personal possessions have been lost. We could also remember that, during the Second World War, many families lost their homes and all their possessions in the German bombing raids. They had no option but to be stoic.

* * *

I do have one suggestion of how some young people could be rescued from a life of crime. Both I, and a probation officer I knew, found that most young criminals, if seen on their own, could be reasoned with and would take on board arguments about how mending their ways would be in their own best interests. However, the moment they were re-united with their peer group, any good resolutions vanished and they went straight back into their old ways.

This was straightforward peer group pressure. It would have taken immense strength and courage to stand apart and refuse to join in the drinking, drug abuse, and burgling or whatever they and their friends got up to. I am convinced that at least a few would genuinely have liked to make a fresh start.

On a national basis, if there could be a database of families, hopefully with boys and girls of a similar age, who were prepared to, effectively, foster these kids and give them a home in a different part of the country where they would be away from the previous bad influences, a new beginning really could be offered.

There would have to be the agreed decision that there should be no contact – certainly in terms of visiting – between the boy or girl attempting to make the most of the opportunity and the old buddies. The new family would have to be welcoming and tolerant – and absolutely not likely to learn bad ways from the newcomer. But I really do feel that this approach would be worth a try. Remuneration given to the host families should, I think, be reasonably generous – not generous enough to make it tempting purely on financial grounds – and I think could be an excellent investment from the country's point of view.

The cost of crime, if one totted up police and court time – on the relatively rare occasions when a criminal is arrested – the sums paid out by insurance companies, working hours lost because of the victims' injury or distress, and I am sure other hidden expenses must be immense. . . but one cannot put a monetary value on the life of a young person being turned around so that it can become productive and meaningful.

THE QUALITIES OF LEADERSHIP

There are leaders of all sorts of groups – from the heads of families to the heads of nations. . . what should be their character traits. . . ? in practice what influences people to choose their leaders. . . ? do the right men get to the top. . . ? and how. . . ? what constitutes genuine status in human terms. . .

What are the qualities that are needed in a leader? These would apply to someone who was the head of any sort of group, from the husband and father of the family, to those running their own small businesses, the heads of large corporations and organizations, and governments.

They need to be able to exercise judgement – judgement which is wise and which will command respect. Respect can only exist if it has been earned – and it can only be earned if the leader has demonstrated that he is a good man of sound, honest character, who is aware of the needs of those his decisions and actions will affect and who, if it came to it, would put their requirements above his own.

Ideally he should be at ease with all men, communicating easily and naturally in a way that comes from the heart. Modest, but with a sense of responsibility, he would be surprised at how many of the people under his charge loved him. Love would be something he was neither expecting nor seeking – his aim would just be to do his best for all concerned.

The physical appearance of this leader would have no relevance at all. Any initial reaction to good looks or ugliness, a stature tall or short, would soon be overridden by an acknowledgement of the leader's character, which would earn him a sneaking regard from even the most sceptical and hostile of those who saw themselves as his subordinates – and he would see as worthwhile members of his group.

This is not a man who came to the top by elbowing the opposition out of the way or by cheating or lying. He would be incapable of being anything other than honest and open in all his dealing. An awareness that all people were valuable, worthy of being given care and consideration, would be so deeply engrained in him that any other concept would be unimaginable.

* * *

What sort of people make it to the top in the world today? In exercising our judgement – the judgement which put them there – we have lost the plot. The winners in today's world are not chosen because, along with an ability to accept authority, they can be relied upon to exercise good, sound, moral judgement and be impartial in their decisions. No – we have been got at by the media and now see a slick appearance as attractive. It is worse than that – for the cut of an expensive suit or flashy tie will be admired while the snake-like (with apologies to snakes) calculating, self-seeking, greed, any-means-justifies-the-end-if-it-keeps-me-in-power look in the eyes goes un-noticed, at least by the majority.

Theses horrible characteristics can manifest in leaders in all circumstances. The heads of some families revel in their little brief authority by inflicting their own reign of terror, beating their wives and bullying their children. They have it in their power to make the lives of a small number of people absolute hell.

All the more necessary, then, that leaders who can wield their power over greater numbers of people should be well fitted to their role – and being well-fitted means having the human qualities which ensure that any decisions taken are not influenced by arrogance – the expediency of ensuring that benefits continue to go to him or herself at the expense of the more vulnerable majority.

What has put these odious people in power? Vanity – it is

their success at putting forward an image. Appearance is all-important. On the whole anyone without good looks who has reached the top has done so aided by a show of wealth – real or imagined. Charismatic or wealthy people have a following – of others who want to be like them, and like them for all the wrong reasons.

Carried along on the crest of a materialistic wave, driven by blind ambition, there is no room for valuing the qualities of human decency. These dare not be contemplated – they would provide a completely incompatible mindset.

* * *

Because we all, at our hearts, have an awareness of what we should be – call it conscience if you like – contemplating how we should be motivated and how we are can be extremely uncomfortable for those who are deliberately following a path which destroys or damages others while it enhances them, their wealth, and their personal standing. I mean, by this, their personal standing as seen by themselves and the probably equally odious hangers-on. In truth they have no status so far as the true human qualities are concerned.

A lady who, kindly, dishes out lunches to children in a little village school for a few pounds a week has more true status that a man worth millions whose path to the top has been achieved through dishonesty, scheming, and caring nothing for the hurt and damage to others that he has caused en route.

DEATH OF DEMOCRACY AND BUREAUCRACY

Democracy and other methods of government. . . how it works and fails. . . how it can become a bureaucracy. . . government interference in many departments. . . the results of this. . . how did this situation come about. . . ? Whatever our leaders do we must stay on track and live our own lives honourably. Is it true that evil leaders are wholly bad. . . or that those we adulate are wholly good? The nanny state has brought about many restrictions through health and safety and other laws. . . the stupidity of some rules is almost beyond belief.

Democracy has been described as the best of the options of the bad systems of government which are on offer. Certainly, if one looks historically at the actions of men who have made themselves dictators, one can discount that choice. Hitler, Stalin, Che Guevara, Mao Tse Tung, Robert Mugabe, Idi Amin, all have been guilty of terrible things as their egotism knew no bounds, and the only people around them kept in their positions by going along with whatever destructive and evil course of action the dictator proposed.

* * *

Traditionally, Great Britain has regarded itself as having a democratic, and democratically elected, government. The prime minister did not have it all his own way. He referred matters to the members of his cabinet. All decisions were, at least in theory, taken after considered and mature discussions among a group of well-informed men, who respected each others' opinions and judgement.

And what about the electoral process? Proportional representation must be the fairest method of electing members of parliament, but it was regarded as impractical. It was felt over the years that in order for governments to be in a position to make and carry out their decisions they must have a majority of seats in parliament. By elected representatives coming from specific constituencies it was far more likely that there would be overall majorities. However, in a close-run election it was perfectly possible that the numbers of the electorate voting for the party ending up as the opposition would be greater that that who had supported those who ended up in power. This was the case when Tony Blair won his third election. In fact more of the electorate voted for the Conservatives than Labour.

It was also the commonly held belief that George Bush won the vote in Florida, during his first campaign, by trashing the votes of coloured people – identified by their names – classifying them as criminal or insane, and therefore not eligible to vote.

* * *

While in power UK governments can influence the likely outcome of future elections by tinkering with the boundaries of the electoral constituencies. Politicians have a pretty good idea how people in various parts of the country are likely to vote, so they can manipulate things to their own advantage.

Whether a democracy remains as one, or slowly but surely turns into a bureaucracy will largely depend on the laws passed by the government. The more controlling it becomes – interfering increasingly in education, health, legal, and other systems – the more undemocratic it will tend to become.

On the whole the specialists in these systems are not the government or their so-called advisers, but headmasters, doctors and nurses, and members of the police force who have sound grass roots knowledge gained from many years of experience in their respective fields. A good government will stand back, credit them with knowing what they are doing, and leave them to get on with it.

* * *

I – and I think many others – feel that around the beginning of the twenty-first century the prime minister showed signs of being a control freak. An obsession with producing statistics meant that those dealing with crime, examination results, and National Health Service patients had to produce figures to – allegedly – confirm that they were doing a good job, and were improving all the time.

This approach had anything but the desired effect. With unreasonable and unjustified pressure being put on those who were probably working well anyway the tendency to massage those figures – in just the same way that the government would massage its own to ingratiate itself in the public – became irresistibly attractive. Anything to get an interfering government off their backs!

The results so far as the public were concerned could be quite disastrous. I heard personally from people waiting for medical appointments whose names disappeared from lists just before the deadlines after which the delay would have earned them a governmental black mark.

My own husband – being admitted to hospital for the last time – was suddenly removed from the accident and emergency department into a corridor – had he been there a couple more minutes the four-hour rule would have been breached and the hospital would have again had a cross in the failing box.

I discovered that if someone wanted to report a crime the police did everything in their power to deter this – to avoid, I have no doubt, an increase in the figures for unsolved crimes.

The government's desire to push more and more youngsters into university – whether they were suitable or not – coincided, if I remember correctly, with a time when youth unemployment figures looked bad and were likely to get worse.

In none of these instances did government policy have anything but an adverse effect on the public. Their only justification – if it could be called that – was to make the prime minister look good in his own eyes. The whole policy of being dictated to through statistics was, I feel sure, to provide 'facts' to woo the electorate – to kid them things were very much better than they actually were.

* * *

How did all this come about? I would attribute it to the 'presidential' style of the prime minister Blair, which denied members of the cabinet their traditional input of possibly much more sound ideas about how the country should be run. We were at the mercy of Mr. Arrogant – and I do not see Mr. Arrogant as a man who had sound judgement.

In human terms this caused much suffering to many. Teachers already struggling with the demands made upon them were faced with more and more administration. They had gone into their profession to teach children. Some of the children, not naturally academic or from homes that would not encourage a good attitude to education, were bound to fail, but if too many did the finger of blame was pointed at the members of staff and head teachers.

The police had pressure on them so that it must appear they were getting on top of knife, gun, and other violent crimes – rather that being able to go out onto the streets where they were needed they had to waste time with paperwork.

In the first half of 2010 there was a report showing that a couple of police forces had reached the point here they had more administrative officers on their payrole than policemen and women. This pattern of government-inflicted stupidity invaded countless situations, solving nothing, wasting time, and generally producing bogus figures. The overall effect was that the public suffered – the energy which should have gone into serving them was wasted rather than being applied where it was needed most.

* * *

Flying in the face of the millions that demonstrated against the war in Iraq was the most gross and unforgivable example of sneering at public opinion.

On a very much smaller scale another demonstration was dealt with to my way of thinking – inappropriately. A Free Tibet group assembled outside the Chinese Embassy in London. Reports were that those supporting the cause were treated harshly, and were quickly sent on their way. Why? I later heard that Blair was playing host to Rupert Murdoch, and Rupert Murdoch had a Chinese wife. Must get our priorities right! Yet more sneering at the right-minded public.

Will it ever be possible to reclaim the less imperfect method of government that we once had? Will reasonable discussion among people who are very much less egocentric and far more altruistic be able to return as the vehicle of government? We can only hope so. But whatever happens it is up to us to reject totally the example set by those who erroneously consider themselves superior to us, and lead lives which show we have the honour that they have not.

Is it true that all these terrible leaders do lack all traces of humanity? Are there indications that even they are capable of love and kindness?

Stalin the brutal Soviet dictator wanted to rid the world of the Ukrainian nation. In his attempt to achieve this he created a man-made famine, and millions starved as his troops and secret police raided the villages taking their crops and the food from their homes.

But Stalin's daughter described how he had been a good and kind father. The gulf between how he ran his private family life and his government must have been immense.

Radovan Karadizic, the Bosnian Serb leader, wanted to

answer charges of crimes against humanity, was in hiding for years. When eventually caught it was discovered he had taken on the persona of a benevolent old man offering support and complementary therapies to his patients. Completely unaware of his past they had found him to be a spiritual and meditative man, of whom they had grown fond.

Conversely, are those generally regarded as wonderful really as un-flawed as many would like to believe? Many years before the second world war, when Churchill was pursuing an earlier career he described any soldier who did not want to use chemical warfare against the Iraqis as 'squeamish'.

* * *

The advent of the nanny state has resulted in all kinds of restrictions which a few years ago would have been openly regarded as preposterous and ignored. Bureaucracy has gone crazy.

A dictatorial attitude has filtered down through our systems, with preposterous results. A child taking a birthday cake baked by her great grandmother for the girl's ninth birthday and taken to school to be shared with her friends returned home uneaten. It was held to be too unhealthy to be handed round the class. . . Have we gone mad? I think we have.

Extreme health and safety laws dictated that the emergency services would not use their ladders and ropes down a steep 15 foot high bank to rescue someone drowning in 18 inches of water at the bottom. Police community officers watched a ten-year-old drown in a lake – they no longer have to be able to swim. Should we help?

Jo Public, legally speaking, would be ill advised to interfere. Should he go to someone's aid, he could later be sued if a case could be made out for him having inflamed an injury. Fine, if the victim can be left where he is. What if he is in a car which is on fire? I would rather be dragged unceremoniously through a window, even if a bit more damage was done, than being left to burn. Common sense has vanished.

* * *

Criminal checks to ensure that paedophiles do not have the opportunity to get near children have now reached the point where granny is no longer allowed to have a few photographs of a child's school sports day.

We have almost reached the stage where Mr and Mrs Average are assumed to be a threat to children unless they can be proved innocent through police databases. Activities like taking a group of kids out of school hours to a football match organized by volunteers must be viewed with suspicion, no matter that all the parents are happy with what may have been a long-standing arrangement.

These extreme measures will not, unhappily, result in people having lesser injuries or, probably, fewer children being abused. Most paedophiles are members of the immediate family or friends. They will, however, stifle spontaneous and altruistic behaviour.

I know of one young couple who were not allowed to take their much-wanted little baby home from the maternity unit unless they produced a suitable car seat for the ride home. They did not possess a car.

I think that says it all.

The American And European Diseases

The United Kingdom has been encouraged to see the United States as a shining example. . . is this so. . . ? some Americans appear to be prosperous at the expense of others. . . there is the tradition that the poor cannot have medical treatment if they cannot afford it. . . do the people there show their humanity. . . ? are some of their rich greedy as well. . . ? does competition for position get out of hand. . . ? is life valued, particularly that of poor people in other countries. . . from America we have caught the sue everyone for anything culture, which has had a huge negative knock-on effect. Europe has also affected our way of life. . . laws passed in Brussels apply to us although our MPs have not considered them. . . unrestricted travel between countries has been a mixed blessing. . . for years there were stupid and destructive rules concerning the growing and marketing of fruit and vegetables.

In the same way that families can be influenced by others around them, or villages by the surrounding neighbourhood, so countries can be influenced by other countries, with the apparently less successful wanting to grow like those that are more prosperous.

Successive political leaders have tried to encourage a special relationship with the United States seeing this as somehow attracting kudos to themselves and enhancing the international status of Great Britain.

Before getting close to or imitating anything the object of admiration should be studied closely to see if it is worthy of adulation. The term The Great American Dream gets flashed around, possibly because as a new country it saw itself as not carrying the baggage of history and traditions of older nations. It could be argued that the dream started by stealing land which had belonged to the native Indian population for countless generations, and butchering them.

America certainly has the most materialistic aims and ambitions which it has, for many of its nationals, fulfilled. There is a very wide gap, however, between how the middle class white and the poor black populous have been living. Hopefully, this situation may improve with the advent of a black president, although when he wanted to ensure that anyone needing health care could get it, no matter how poor, he met with a great deal of hostile opposition.

American systems were based on privately run insurance companies and those participating feared that their expensively-funded policies would be jeopardised. Their system had been set up so that the relatively rich could get what they wanted, and anyone who could not afford it could go to the wall. It had been seen as acceptable that the unfunded could die on the hospital steps.

When hurricane Katrina hit an area mostly inhabited by poor black people the devastation remained for years. Everyone knew that had the disaster affected people Bush and his cronies saw as worthwhile help would have been swift. Instead, there were many reports of insurance companies wriggling out of their commitments and getting away with it. Theses people had no one prepared to fight for them.

There were reports that one rescue team who went to the area refused to help a group of stranded girls unless they raised their shirts and flashed their breasts. When they refused they were left where they were.

In sharp contrast the reaction of people in the poorer parts of the world where the tsunami struck showed their spontaneous humanity. Families who survived came forward to offer homes to children who had been orphaned.

In which sort of country would your rather live?

* * *

Being rich does not stop people being greedy. When a store in a relatively prosperous part of America opened its door at the start of a sale a woman was, literally, trampled to death.

Again, by contrast, we have seen newsreels of many starving people in the third world countries patiently queuing for their daily rations of food – upon which the lives of them and their families depend.

* * *

There have been accounts of the parents of teenagers who are competing to become cheerleaders resorting to just about anything to sabotage the opponents' chances.

So much for children being loved for themselves. True American values!

Predictably the lives of people in other countries – particularly poor ones – count for nothing.

In December 1984 the American company Union Carbide was responsible for the escape of isocyanate gas over Bhopal, in a poor part of India. The death toll was 2,500, and 100,000 were homeless. Decades later no compensation had been given. There were, however, winners – American lawyers made a fortune out of taking sides and representing the company or the people.

In December 2009 there were reports that a poison was still leaking into the water used by the people, and that carbon tetracloride was 1,000 times above acceptable levels. There were horrendous birth defects reported. A woman of 22 had the body of a 12-year old, and she was relatively lucky.

In June 2010 there was an attempt at 'justice'. However, and predictably (he was, after all, rich and American and not poor and Indian) the American former chairman of Union Carbide's India operations who was briefly arrested after the incident was declared to have absconded, and refused to return to face the charges. Seven executives, however, all Indian, were each sentenced to two years in jail, but planned to appeal.

There was an estimate that, after the incident, 100,000 people received just under £3 per month compensation for a brief period. Sufferers experienced cancer, blindness, immune system, breathing, and neurological problems and birth defects.

* * *

In Brazil for many years the police were able to gun down the street children as though they were vermin. If there was a fuss, and someone had to face a charge, it was not regarded as serious.

* * *

The re-building of Iraq was taking forever. . . again, the welfare of poor non-Americans was seen as low priority. Corruption was rife and it was the people who suffered.

* * *

What 'goodies' have we won by becoming more like our cousins across the pond?

We have now acquired a culture in which opportunists – most of whom fall into the lower orders who prefer not to work for their money or the very rich who will chase money in any way possible – will look for any excuse to rush to a solicitor and sue anyone who might be held to have damaged them in any way. Accidents at work, or on behalf of children who take a tumble in the playground – who among us didn't, and it didn't harm us either – are seen as fair game.

No one would deny that the concept of being able to claim damages is a good one – in appropriate circumstances. But things have got completely out of control both from the point of view of the trivia on which some solicitors hope to increase their customer base, and the huge sums which are awarded in some instances.

The result of this – the threat of being sued if minor, everyday events go wrong – has been decidedly negative. Those in charge of children no longer dare let them do anything which could result in any injury. Scraped knees and the occasional broken bone used to be seen as a natural part of growing up. For the sake of a one-in-a-thousand chance no child is able to enjoy the freedom to learn from and explore the world as his grandparents did.

Claims against the National Health Service – some of which may be justified – mean that there is ever-decreasing money in the pot to treat the ill. If my observations are correct it appears that sometimes individuals did a lot better than those who – as part of a large group - suffered the devastating results of having transfusions of contaminated blood. Justice tends to play second fiddle to expediency in theses cases.

A friend of mine – one of the few survivors of many who had got hepatitis from badly managed blood banks – and her peers waited many years for any kind of compensation. I remember, by contrast, the case of a medical student who sued because she found she could not cope with the sight of blood or needles, and got a very large sum of money.

To my mind the boot should have been on the other foot – she should have had to pay back the country's investment in her training up to that point. Anyone planning to be a doctor but who is squeamish in this way should never have embarked on the course.

* * *

Public events are now very restricted because it is difficult to find insurance companies prepared to give cover for third party liability. I know of one group of handicapped people whose major event of the year – competing among a line of decorated floats – had to be discontinued.

Art exhibitions have also had problems. One group believed they had cover but later discovered that only paintings attached to the wall were acceptable. Anything three-dimensional, to include such crafts items as jewellery, rendered their policy null and void.

When an employee of a small company had an accident – most people would have regarded this as attributable to his own stupidity – he saw the opportunity to sue, and the firm only just managed to stay in business. The get-rich-quick merchant had no care as to whether his ex-colleagues would be left without jobs.

Another good way to make money is to grossly exaggerate the effect of the mishap. Malingerers who have been in car crashes are more than likely to milk their injuries for all they are worth, resulting in the cost of insurance rising for everyone else and inconveniencing people in their places of work who have to cover for them.

* * *

In America a woman whose dentist extracted thirteen of her teeth by mistake was awarded £1.4 million in damages.

Mickey Mouse money is now featuring in claims being made in the UK. There were reports that a city lawyer was in line for a £12 million record payout for a breakdown which followed sexual discrimination and harassment. Another city firm was being sued by an accountant for 30 million euros for a sex and racial harassment case which resulted in hurt feelings.

However, a rape victim claiming from the Criminal Injuries Compensation Board received £3,300. A 'different kind of rape' could have attracted £11,000.

A gay security guard received £62,500 saying he was depressed because a colleague had wobbled her breasts at him provocatively.

Soldiers returning from Iraq or Afghanistan – who are

sometimes terribly injured with limbs missing and facing lives that will be changed for ever – are, like the rape victim, dependent on claims which come from government funding.

The Ministry of Defence has fifteen categories for military injury. These range from a top handout of £570,000 down to £1,115.

A soldier who had been shot was offered £9,250 and his proposed £48,000 tribunal award was being fought by the Ministry of Defence.

Moral – steer clear of rapists, you are on to a doubly bad deal.

Moral – don't get injured fighting in a war, but do take offence if there is nastiness at work. You could end up very rich indeed.

* * *

How about Europe? Has this brought us great blessings? The cost of running the European Parliament is high – British MPs who manage to become our representatives in Brussels are in clover. What has the British tax-payer got out of it?

Ted Heath took the country into the European Economic Comunity – at the time there was no political party seriously opposing the move – and the Conservative Government agreed that laws passed in Brussels would automatically apply in the U.K. without having to be considered by our MPs. The implications of this have been enormous and not to our advantage.

The vexed problem of human rights – so good in some instances and so preposterous in others – has resulted, in the eyes of many, in the wrong people being favoured. Most people feel that immigrants who commit murder should be deported, but some are allowed to stay because their 'human rights' would be violated if they were parted from their families who are here. There is no place in this argument for considering the families of the victims these criminals have murdered.

The automatic right of European Union citizens to travel between countries seeking work has been a very mixed blessing. Racial harmony has not exactly been enhanced as droves of immigrants, some temporary and some not, have come into the country and undercut the wages of the local workforce. There has been the popular conception or misconception that foreigners are also bent on abusing the benefits, housing, and health systems. The whole process appears to be totally out of control.

* * *

Uniformity was an obsession with many members of the European Parliament. Fields of wonderful species of English apples were trashed because they did not conform. Fruit and vegetables had to be a particular size and shape. When the credit crunch started one man with a fruit stall had to destroy a complete consignment of kiwi fruit as they were considered too small. He was not even allowed to give them away to poor families struggling to feed their children. About the middle of 2009 this stupid rule finally bit the dust, but not before an enormous amount of harm had been done.

* * *

The EEC started out as a small and rather select group of countries which formed the European Union. One of the founding principles was that all citizens would be free to move and work in any other member country. At the beginning the average citizens of these countries would have been able to fit in well as they moved across the borders.

At first there was no great immigration or emigration as the nations involved were, in general terms, equally prosperous with similar opportunities and standards of living. There was little to lure people from one country to another. Culturally, too, there were definite similarities.

However, as more and more countries joined the community found itself opening its borders to people from very different cultural and economic backgrounds. The situation changed considerably and, predictably, problems arose. Those who perceive themselves to be disadvantaged and under privileged will naturally be tempted to try their luck elsewhere if the opportunity arises.

Many of these migrants were good people who could be welcomed. Some were not. A woman who was the victim of a pickpocket – she took savings which were to have been spent on Christmas presents – reported the matter to the police. She was told that they were aware of gangs of east Europeans who would go to a town or city and target the people there for the day before returning to wherever they were living. The police knew exactly what was happening, but they appeared powerless to stop it.

These are exactly the sort of incidents which breed anger and resentment. They also tend to blacken – quite unjustly – the reputations of others from their countries in the eyes of the native populous.

There will always be people in whose interests it is to move from country to country in order to evade the law in the place where they have been living. Many a very dodgy Englishman has moved to the Costa del Crime – attracted by the lack of an extradition agreement between England and Spain.

WARS

*Wars are vile. . . how did the public feel about the war in Iraq. . . ?
how does America fit in. . . ? what about Afghanistan. . . ? no war is
worth a single human life. . . it is politicians who start them, not people
generally. . . politicians remain well away from the killing. . . is a
war the way to stop the actions of an evil president or leader of a
country. . . ? Iraq – a war fought against the wishes of most of the
British people. . . how did Blair justify this. . . ? but extreme
suffering does bring out wonderful qualities in those who are victims and
those who try to help them. We get an edited version of the damage we
are doing to the other side.*

War is the ultimate and most vile illustration of what happens
when those who hold controlling power set aside any human
decency they may once have had, and decide to start a war.

What were the feelings of the public in the run up to the
invasion of Iraq?

One day I got out of the car, which displayed anti-war
posters. An Arab stopped me. He was very quiet and polite,
and almost in tears, 'Thank you, thank you, there must be
another way. . . ' At that time his homeland and family were
under threat. In a short time they may well have been dead –
their cities had been devastated.

I made an anti-war piece of sculpture from items including
a broken mug, bent fork, charred electric plug and lead, a bit
of a damaged car, a broken brick, and part of a burnt shoe
with a hint of dark red around it. A small girl showed a lot of
interest, and I explained how I had tried to represent all the
aspects of life which had been destroyed. I added, 'The most
evil thing you can do is to invent reasons to start a war.' I had
become aware of her mother, standing a little way off. She
spoke,'I do so agree with you.'

'What do you think. . . ?' Americans who usually phoned

only on birthdays or at Christmas were on the line. I responded, 'I would rather that Bush, Blair, and all their war-mongering cronies were towed into the middle of the Atlantic and sunk rather than one innocent Iraqi life was lost.' There was a pause, and sigh of relief, 'I am so glad we agree about this.'

A 'posh' friend, a Queens Counsellor who had known the Blairs well, since before they got married, came to visit. I expressed my views to him as I had to the Americans, expecting him to leap to the prime minister's defence. Instead he came over to me quietly and said, 'I agree with you.' I was so pleased that he confirmed he was the kind and good man I had always believed him to be.

He along with many other barristers known to the Blairs – and members of Cherie Blair's family – took part in London's main anti-war march, the largest demonstration ever seen in the capital. One of them remarked, 'Tony is in trouble. We are here, and we are his friends.'

Sadly, he was wrong. It was not Tony who was in trouble, but the 800,000 Iraqis who were to die in the hostilities, and the estimated three million refugees who fled their devastated cities.

* * *

Americans have never experienced a proper war in which their civilians suffered the immediacy of the blitz. Fighting has been done safely overseas with only servicemen being at risk. London, and the major cities of almost all nations involved in conflict, have first-hand knowledge of invasion by bombs, rockets, or tanks.

September 11th was the closest America has ever come to this. Terrible though the atrocity was the numbers concern were tiny compared with the casualties of war.

The destruction of the twin towers was a statement by the killers condemning extreme greed and wealth, the methods by which America exerted – and abused – its power in the world. Its control of monetary systems, and unwanted interference as it tried to control the way other countries were run, attracted enormous resentment.

The method of the demonstration was terrible, but the cause was much more understandable.

This may have been a terrorist action, but Iraq had nothing whatever to do with it. In fact Saddam was among the most secular of the Arab leaders. Historically, going back before Iraq invaded Kuwait, he was regarded as an ally by the west.

I do not believe that the destruction of the twin towers should have been seen as the overture to a time when extremists and their bombs would become commonplace as a terrifying feature of American and European life. However, we shall never know as Bush and Blair must have become the finest recruiting agents that the terrorists could have wished for, and the political scene was changed.

I feel the danger at home may have increased – the situation further fuelled by the protestations of those who led the war against Iraq for ever trying to, in this case retrospectively, justify it.

What about Afghanistan? In my opinion this is yet another place where our troops are, but should not be.

All we should have done in Afghanistan was to destroy crops of opium poppies, compensating handsomely the farmers whose families would have starved had they not been so employed, and then paid them a king's ransom regularly for producing good healthy food. Thousands of lives would have been saved, and many billions of pounds.

I also feel (this is complete cloud cuckoo land, and I accept it as such) that we should scrap our armed forces. If you gave a child an air gun for Christmas and instead of shooting at safe targets he tried to kill off all the neighbours' cats and dogs you would take it from him. After what we have done in Iraq we have proved that we are not fit to be in control of such power. Similarly, the Americans should have disbanded their armed services after the tragedy of Vietnam. They have learned nothing.

At one time I though that if the U.K. and America became poor enough their governments would no longer be able to afford wars. Before the advent of Barack Obama I think that Bush would have watched his own people starve rather that stop the fighting in just the same way that some African dictators squander the nation's wealth while their countrymen die around them. . .

* * *

'A war is not worth a single life.' These were the wise words of Harry Patch. When he died in July 2009 he was the last surviving soldier from the First World War. For most of his life he had remained silent on the horror he had seen. Badly injured in the battle of Passchendaele he was in fact one of the very lucky ones – 250,000 British soldiers died. As his life drew to a close he started talking about his experiences. At his funeral the song 'Where have all the young men gone?' was selected by his grandson – to emphasize Harry's message of peace and reconciliation.

'Wars are not between people – they are between politicians.' I heard this on Radio 4 and only wish I knew the name of the commentator whom I would like to congratulate.

I would like to suggest (cloud Cuckoo land, I know) that no prime minister or president can declare war unless he also undertakes to put his sons and any other male members of his family and close friends in the front line. If he feels a war is justified lives must be lost and he should demonstrate his acceptance of this by being prepared to lose his own family first. Committing other people's loved ones I see as gross cowardice.

* * *

It is true that some political situations must be stopped. No one could stand by and allow Hitler to exterminate the Jews and invade other countries in Europe as he did. I do wonder however if wars are the answer. Surely the aim should be to get rid of the political leader not slaughter the civilians who happen to be living under his regime. Yes, the Germans voted Hitler into power. From their point of view he had put their country back on its feet, financially speaking. After the war was over, when they had to accept what had been done in their name, many were terribly ashamed – and rightly so. Was our saturation bombing of Dresden and other cities justified? It was ordinary families that were targeted not Hitler or the S.S.

* * *

Now back to Iraq.

This book has no wish to concern itself with 'religion'. In fact that word would never have seen the light of print had it not been for the fact that messrs Blair and Bush – particularly the former – waxed lyrical about their conviction that they were doing the 'right' thing when deciding to go to war against Iraq.

This book judges that decision in the light of the fact that all men are equal human beings, with a right to exist peacefully, free from attack by others. However the Prime Minister and President – again, particularly the former – declare themselves to be avid Christians and it would not be unreasonable to suppose that they were guided in their actions by their religion.

Strange. . . both the Archbishop of Canterbury and the Pope never wavered in being totally opposed to the war. Did Mr Blair have a direct line to Jesus Christ, or God, or both, which the Archbishop and the Pope were denied? My simple and perhaps rather obvious definition of a Christian would be one who accepts the teachings of Christ as being 'right' and of trying to follow them.

173

Jesus was born a Jew, so he accepted the Ten Commandments, which include the words, 'Thou shalt not kill'. Just that. No exceptions for wanting to get your hands on someone else's oil or hoping to go down in history as a great war leader. But Jesus himself had more to say on the subject of how we should treat our enemies. We are told to offer the other cheek. Far from killing them, we should 'love our enemies.'

I would suggest that the poor Iraqis were in no way even our enemies. They were simply the inhabitants of an Arab country being governed by an evil man although, it could be argued, possibly no more evil that some of the leaders of African nations around at the same time. And, of course, they were sitting on oil wells.

Back to the vexed subject of 'religion'. If, as he appeared to imply, Blair believed that the message he received – from God, or Christ, or both – that it was 'right' to go to war against the Iraqis then we are all invited also to believe that Jesus's teachings which have lasted for 2,000 years, and the Jewish teachings which are older still – have been overturned, although the Archbishop and the Pope were kept in the dark about it.

I personally feel that this is nonsense – and a particularly unpleasant nonsense at that. I believe that people should be at liberty to follow any religion or belief system that they choose – and I also believe that those religions have the right not to be grossly misrepresented.

If some scruffy homeless beggar planned to kill people because he heard God telling him to he would certainly not be moved into Downing Street, but end his days in a secure unit for his own safety and that of others.

If we are to accept that Blair is sane, and was responsible for his own decisions, then my opinion is that there will be no justice in this world until he and Bush stand before an international court to answer charges of war crimes, and crimes against humanity.

While the then – and now almost forgotten – leader of the Conservatives and former soldier Iain Ducan-Smith supported Blair's decision to go to war right-minded members of the British public spontaneously demonstrated against it in numbers never previously witnessed.

I believe this is one of the most atrocious examples of bureaucracy annihilating democracy. So much for Blair's 'presidential' style of government.

* * *

Of course, from the political viewpoint, the electorate in Britain had to be fed a censored version of what was happening as much as possible. Never mind the loss of mere life – votes depended on it.

The official government figures of Iraqis killed stayed – for years literally – at 100,000 – 150,000. Medical organizations in that country did their own estimate based on average statistics, and said the number could be one million. In 2009 final accurate figures were produced by the Iraqi authorities and came to 800,000. There were reputed to be three million refugees.

While the war was in progress I heard an interview with an Iraqi doctor, who was working at a hospital, on the 5pm Radio 4 News. He described the lack of water and electricity and medicaments. He explained that because the tank-busters used by the Americans and British had depleted uranium on their tips more and more patients were suffering from cancer, but his hospital had none of the drugs they needed, and security was so bad that there could be no travelling between hospitals by patients or medical personnel.

Dear oh dear, the British public must not know about this. The same recording was played at 6pm on Radio 4, and on the 10pm TV news. But there was one notable omission – the statements about the depleted uranium on the tank-busters and the resulting cancer cases had been deleted.

Anyone who doubts the damage we did to the civilians in Iraq - who like Blair and David Miliband, feel we should just 'move on' as though the atrocity has become no more than a political inconvenience to themselves - should have tuned in to the BBC on 4 March 2010. There was a harrowing account of how, during the war near Fallujah, our allied forces bombed buildings, sending them into a river which supplied the Iraqis with drinking water.

All evidence pointed to horribly contaminated drinking water causing many children to be born with deformatives. These ranged from the relatively minor - children with six fingered hands and six-toed feet - to the almost umimaginable including a baby with three heads. Many had missing arms and legs, brain damage, and paralysis. All three children of one woman were severly handicapped.

Official advice to women living in the area is that they should not get pregnant. What more of an admission do you want than this? American law ensures that compensation claims cannot be made by civilians, like these, whose injuries were the result of military conflict.

There is nothing new about the public being lied to for political convenience. During the Gulf War – when Iraq invaded Kuwait – we were fed computerised pictures of smart bombs being targeted at specific locations on T.V. news programmes. Wonderful, fantastic new technology, the civilians would be spared. Many years later, when the true facts had to be made available, it was admitted that no more than one in a hundred of these bombs actually reached its mark. The rest landed, as always, on suffering civilians.

* * *

While I want no one to be killed or injured I have more sympathy for any civilian that for anyone in uniform. Servicemen have chosen to be involved, and are prepared to kill. Civilians want to go about their daily business, unarmed, and hurt no one.

I doubt if 'good' ever comes out of war – but I cannot stress too strongly that the extreme suffering it causes often brings out the very best in people.

There is a reason for this. Left only with the clothes they were wearing, their homes, schools, places of employment gone, those who survived the blitz in London and the other major cities found truly wonderful love, friendship, and support among those who could offer them any help.

One branch of my family lost everything – everything material, that is – and were left, four homeless ladies and a cat in a basket. Hearing of their plight a friend who still had a roof over her head offered them shelter. She hated cats, so my family thanked her but declined. She was horrified! Of course the cat was welcome too! What were they thinking of!

When all our worldly goods are taken from us we are forced to live with the only thing we are left with – our humanity - the one real and meaningful thing that we all possess. The concept of sharing takes on a new and immediate meaning. Hunger is ignored if there is a small, sick child whose need for what little food there is is greater.

Television footage of the devastated cities of Iraq echoed the London blitz, although I think the British were much more efficient at restoring some sort of water supply for the survivors. Reports indicated that the Iraqis remained without water or electricity for very protracted periods. How any of them survived is a miracle.

* * *

Not many people now have personal memories of the blitz. What was it like? As a small child I used to visit Bristol regularly. In the early 1950s it was a city with lots of parking spaces – green areas of land – and craters one had to avoid. These had been front gardens and basement rooms, where once children played and grandparents visited for Sunday tea. . . the body parts, the shards of glass, the torn remnants of curtains had long since been cleared away. . .

Any who see the effects of war on their fellow men can only feel deeply saddened. The wish – that politicians should learn from these gross and devastating mistakes – remains only a wish. What motivates them? Is it the desire for even more power – taking control over a country which is not their own? Do they envisage that a military victory will enhance their own standing no matter what the circumstances? Have they built up some unreasonable feeling of hatred against people who happen to be the nationals of another country?

Whatever the motive they have, it outweighs, in their warped minds, the cost of many thousands of good, clean, honest human lives – the decent run-of-the-mill people whom they obviously despise and fail to value. People who, in human terms, are worth a million of them.

SERVICEMEN

Servicemen – why do they choose that career? If he is told to kill he must. . . there is no place for his own judgement. . . through their actions some become brutalised while others live with the guilt of what they have done. . . they lead the un-real lives of those who are taken care of and may be unable to cope in civvy street when discharged... one man however, a saint-like figure, devoted his life to helping servicemen ridden with guilt at the killings and maimings for which they had been responsible.

There are obvious attractions to joining the armed forces. A lad who has had no more than an average education will find himself with a regular income, and no worries about getting accommodation or being fed or clothed. He has the prospect of going abroad with all arrangements taken care of. There is the romance of being seen as a hero, representing his country.

Few will seriously contemplate the possibility of being killed when they enlist. They are far more likely to hone in on tales in the papers of young men being lauded for their acts of valour, or at a humbler level to be able to impress their families and friends with stories of their lives overseas.

To their families they are likely to be greeted as heroes, even if in reality the roles they have played have been mundane and tedious rather than those involving excitement and danger. Can simply enlisting qualify someone to be viewed as a hero? Most join up because they are convinced that the services will provide them with the lifestyle they would enjoy, in the same way that most people apply for jobs which they believe will give them pleasure.

The dead are always seen as heroes. They have given their lives sometimes completely in vain, the term friendly fire applied to circumstances when, unintentionally, their own side killed them. If the word heroes brings comfort to their

179

families no-one would deny them – but there are now bereaved parents who see that their sons died in wars that were never justified, and face what I would see as the truth, that death on the battlefield is not glorious, but wrong.

* * *

So much for the recruitment of the squaddie. The officer class are generally drawn from a different strata of society. Educated at good academic schools and with academic university degrees behind them many train at Sandhurst before taking command of other men. On the whole these favoured beings are at far less risk of being killed than the canon fodder serving under them. If there are incidents whey tend to pick up medals.

Quite often there is a history of military service in the family – predisposing a favourable attitude. In good times there will be a very good income, guaranteed pension, foreign travel, a lot of fun, and very little danger. When they have to do the more serious job they were trained for they are seen to rise to the occasion well, having a good relationship with their men, and organizing attacks etc. to the best of their ability.

However, all soldiers act under orders. A soldier who flatly refuses to fight in a war declared by his government because he honestly believes it to be wrong will be court martialled. He is effectively banned from using his own reasonable judgement. If he is told to kill his fellow men he must do so.

There have been accounts of ex-servicemen committing sometimes nasty violent crimes after discharge or while on leave. One possibility is that they have been brutalised or affected mentally, but a friend suggested to me that it simply indicated the sort of people who were attracted to the military life.

Certainly training can be aimed at destroying a serviceman's acceptance that an enemy is also a fellow human being. It was discovered that, in World War II, only 15% of American Marines aimed their guns to kill. The thought of ending another life ran contrary to their deeper and better instincts. Training was altered. Targets no longer looked like men, but were shadowy silhouettes, no longer inviting identification with people. By the time the Marines were fighting in Vietnam 90% were happy to aim accurately and to despatch life without any qualms of conscience.

* * *

In carrying out orders – and sometimes going beyond those orders – soldiers can become brutalised. This is not my opinion, but the opinion of some ex-servicemen speaking out against themselves, regretting publicly some of the acts they committed. They did not see their actions as those of heroes, but recognized them for what they were – cruel and bullying. They gave accounts of methods of torture they had inflicted on the enemy. With repentance they accepted that those people were human beings as they were themselves. They rejected their earlier attitudes.

Some of their peer group, however, continued to believe that the atrocities committed were justified, and they were proud of them. Probably the most widely publicised of the torturers was the American Lynndie England, at the Abu Ghraib prison in Iraq, along with her lover Corporal Charles Graner. Together they forced a line of prisoners to form a line-up, and masturbate, just one of many obscenities they inflicted on their victims. Lynndie England had no regrets, possibly the most chilling fact of all.

However, the remorseful ex-torturers described how they had subjected the captives in their care to sleep deprivation, playing heavy metal during the night, giving potentially fatal electric shocks, subjecting them to extremes of hot and cold – when they were dripping with cold water they would stand them in front of an air conditioner – depriving them of water while keeping them in sweltering heat.

A psychiatrist noted that some torturers simply denied what they had done, and others would be prepared to describe what they saw, but not what they did. Psychologically it was probable that the torturer, at the time, acted to make his victim feel he could destroy him. This counted as success.

* * *

Trauma – a word applied to many different sorts of situations. In the context of war there are two obvious sorts of trauma. One is the horror of seeing, possibly for the first time, the mutilated corpses of one's fellow soldiers. One's best mate can be chatting and joking one minute, and lying a heap of mangled flesh the next. Few are going to appear to get through such experiences unscathed, and any who do will almost certainly have grim delayed reactions later.

While it might be good in military terms to see piles of enemy corpses delight at such spectacles is dependent upon the viewer having abandoned the belief that all people are human beings. In modern warfare members of the armed services account for a tiny percentage of those killed. It is far more likely that the heaps of dead will be comprised of small children, their grandparents, mothers out shopping, sick people in hospitals, and pupils in schools.

Expected, robustly, to look the other way and carry on, the soldier must try to continue with the good work of killing – adding to the carnage he has already witnessed. Possibly, he is starting to have his doubts. . .

In retrospect some servicemen hate themselves for the murders they have committed in the name of King or Queen and country. A good friend of mine never recovered from the part he played. He was an R.A.F. navigator during the Second World War. On his return home he found his mother changed forever – his brothers had been victims through death or injury – and the effect on her was catastrophic.

What Geoff had to come to terms with – or try to come to terms with as he never succeeded - was the fact that, night after night, he and the crew of his plane bombed German cities, killing members of families just like his own. True, most of them - though not all – would have voted Hitler into office but in reality they were also just normal, decent people wanting to have homes and jobs, and bring up their children.

Geoff appeared to have much going for him. He was tall and very presentable, always in work, well spoken and well mannered. But he was a wreck. Constantly haunted by the fact he had caused the same terrible suffering to the German families that they had caused his he resorted to alcohol. He never had a good stable relationship with anyone, and lived in a squalid bed-sitter. Only when he was dying was I, one of his few friends, allowed to visit it – he was so ashamed.

* * *

Physically speaking – and this may be the least of their problems – soldiers are waited upon and taken care of as though they were children. They are fed, clothed, housed, and never have to think about paying a gas or electricity bill. True, conditions in the battlefield can be far worse than basic – squalid, deprived, and extremely uncomfortable, but the squaddie takes no responsibility for any of this. His conditions are all found.

Should he who joined the forces as a young recruit find himself years down the line searching for somewhere to live, applying for a job in civvy street, and going through the motions of every-day living which are second nature to most of us, he can find himself pathetically incapable. For as long as he can remember he has been surrounded by his soldier colleagues, his drinking companions. Now he is frighteningly on his own. If he returns to his family he may be lucky, and this may work out if there has been regular contact over the years – but there will not be the shared history and experiences which are so much a part of normal family life.

I have personally met two ex-servicemen who ended up in cardboard boxes in the street. Alcohol is often seen as the way to cope with life's problems, and this will quickly erode any funds which should help these returning heroes to start their new lives. But Andy and Tony had been urinated upon, and Andy set fire to. . . .

Families may discover that their returning hero has a changed personality, and one which they have difficulty in relating to. He alone has seen much of the world, and possibly bloody scenes which brothers, sisters, parents, if he is married his wife and children, could not possibly begin to imagine. There can be a terrible, tragic, irreconcilable split between them. . . at a time when he needs most support.

* * *

A truly remarkable and wonderful man, a Buddhist monk called Thick Nat Han, lived in Vietnam at the time when it was being attacked by America. A contemplative man of God, he wondered how the Americans could behave as they did, bombing peasants in the fields, and spraying napalm – Asian Orange – onto his people. This vile form of weaponry landed on the skin and caused horrific burns. Survivors were scarred for life.

What lead the Americans to behave this way, he asked himself. They claimed to be Christians. Had Jesus Christ preached murder and destruction? He read the Bible. It said, 'Thou shalt not kill' and 'Love your enemies'. Clearly, the Americans were not following the teachings of their spiritual leader. . .

He though further. Many of the servicemen were very young. They had joined the army imagining themselves to be future heroes by serving their country and being part of the great American dream. He had the compassion to see these people not as evil men, but as tragically misguided. He also understood that many of them would later hate themselves for the part they had played in murdering and maiming innocent peasant farmers.

Thick Nat Han founded Plum Village in France. It can best be described as a place where those being destroyed by their own guilt could quietly understand their situation and begin to see, constructively, that they must continue to lead their lives learning by the mistakes of the past, and do their best to make amends. There was a report of one American soldier, distraught, writing to the monk, and saying that by his 18th birthday he had killed sixty people. What could he do? With the love which only a truly wise man could offer, Thick Nat Han told him to be good to the kids living in his block. . .

What a wonderful example this is. No retribution, no hatred, just an overwhelming understanding of humanity, and the suffering experienced on all sides. It is only by this love that such gross and horrendous situations can begin to be healed.

PART FIVE

THE RESULTS OF LOSING OUR
HUMANITY

My method and motivation in writing this book. . . an example of gross double standards created by the circumstances of war. . . other gross discrepancies between the starving and the over-fed. . . some businesses do not have the restrictions put upon them which they should. . . we have come to see money and longevity as our divine rights. . . appearances are given priority – but sometimes truer values are acknowledged. . . sometimes failure to accept responsibility reaches the point of obscenity. . . as does the egocentric attitude of those who believe they have 'made it'. . . governments apply taxpayers' money with a total disregard for the wishes of those taxpayers. . . the display of the love of money can reach unbelievable proportions. . . those who have inflated opinions of themselves believe they are entitled to whatever they want. . . and they should never be accountable for their incompetance no matter what suffering is caused to other people. . . the children of those who are favoured are also held to have greater importnace and value. . .

When I decided to write this book I started to do research. I ended up with a lot of information gleaned mostly from newspapers, Radio 4 news, and books. Much was negative – the media are more likely to publish stories of bad things happening than good.

This is a positive book about healing and for the most part I did not want to point a finger but to speak in general terms. However, I feel it is valid to use extreme cases where things have gone wrong – some relatively minor, some with huge implications – to illustrate what happens when people follow false values rather than abiding by the human qualities of kindness, honesty, and being aware of the needs of others.

So here goes – I offer a job lot of disasters so that you can judge for yourself whether it is right to take part in the battle to heal society – and the wider society in which we live.

* * *

A book told of the very heart-warming story of an American serviceman who had moved heaven and earth to save a puppy discovered in a deserted building in Iraq. Every rule in the book had to be broken as pets were not allowed etc. etc. but with great perseverance and determination the animal was eventually brought to America.

Did any other dogs feature in the book? In passing it was noted that there were stray animals which had been owned by the dead or left behind by refugees. These were starving. Some of them were eating the raw flesh of the corpses which lay in the streets. While the bodies of the American servicemen were brought home with honour in coffins to be lauded as heroes the Iraqi victims – who were just as much someone's son, daughter, wife, or husband – had been reduced to dog food.

* * *

Positioned as we are, with full stomachs and surrounded by groaning supermarket shelves, it is easy not to appreciate food as we should. We may glibly say that half the world is starving, but we have no real conception of what this means.

Greed, greed, greed – buy two for the price of one, three for the price of two. . . but there are many pensioners and single people who do not want to buy in bulk. In wooing their customers by appealing to their greed supermarkets are doing two things. They are discouraging people from buying what they actually want and, effectively, overcharging anyone who wants a single item.

There is the other aspect, too. Vast quantities of food bought by the public is thrown away, uneaten. The starving in third world countries could probably live for a month on what some of us throw away in a week.

Over the years the idea was voiced that 'mountains' of food produced in the Common Market should, perhaps, be sent abroad where it was needed rather than destroyed. I seem to remember such ideas were found to be impractical.

During and after the Second World War, when there was a considerable shortage of food and very strict rationing, households had to have pig bins. These smelly containers were used to collect any scraps, vegetable peelings, etc., and were collected by council workmen on a very regular basis. They were taken to a depot and the produce boiled until it was thoroughly sterilized – then it had become pig-swill. Ghastly though the process may sound, the fact is that the pigs thrived on it, and an immense amount of edible waste was put to good use.

The starving in some countries would probably give their right arms for such pig-swill. The choice could be between eating it, or death.

* * *

When the love of money rules supreme other considerations fall by the wayside.

The government stood by while companies were allowed to make cold calls to people's homes. This – so far as many were concerned – was unacceptable, but the firms' systems were set so that if there were no callers available who ever answered the phone was met with silence.

Silent phone calls had nasty associations. Was a potential burglar checking on whether the house was empty? Could it be a pervert or disturbed person? Someone who had a grudge against the householder? There was the perception that a silent call implied a threat. This cold-calling system should have been outlawed from the start. Many vulnerable people found them terrifying.

Mobile phones brought sudden and great wealth to the companies producing them when they came on the market. It was predictable, though, that people driving cars were likely to lose all concentration if making or receiving calls. By the time laws were put in place to stop this happening many had decided that this habit was a part of life, and the law was ignored. There were also few efforts made to enforce it. Of course, people died or were seriously hurt as a result, but life is cheap. . .

* * *

When the government was throwing billions and billions of pounds into the economy to rescue banks the Archbishop of Canterbury made the dry observation that such sums were not forthcoming to help those dying in third world countries.

Figures showed that, in 2008, the life expectancy for women in Zimbabwe was 38, and for men 34.

As I write this I have just heard that there is an outcry – some of the drugs used to subdue the more challenging symptoms of Alzheimer's disease may shorten the lives of these patients. Please God, if I get to this stage, let me die quickly, and don't fight to keep me alive. I will have had more than my allotted span already. I do not want to scream at, or use violence towards, carers who are struggling to look after me. My view is completely non-politically correct – but I am entitled to it!

Are the families of those with dementia wanting their protracted survival with their own or the patients' best interests at heart?

* * *

The way in which people see things and describe them often reveals more about the observer that the observed.

A jockey – a relatively less well-known man – had a

brilliant win in a major race. While – hopefully – many would have seen this as an encouraging and refreshing outcome a journalist covering the event had more interest in the jockey's appearance. She spent her time criticizing his teeth, and suggesting that his winnings should be spent on improving them. I was relieved to see that I was not the only one critical of her criticism!

There can be hopeful signs which come out of apparently un-hopeful situations.

When Susan Boyle went in for a talent contest she was ignored as she waited for her turn to sing. Known as Worsel Gummage by her family – she had been the daughter who stayed at home and cared for her parents – she dressed in what she, and many, would have regarded as normal clothes, normal that is for having a casual meal out with friends. Others in the competition had 'risen to the occasion' if you like to describe it as such by appearing in all their finery.

However, when Susan opened her mouth the voice of an angel came forth. So beautiful was it that one of the judges – all credit to the smart young woman – admitted that she had been so moved that she had had tears in her eyes.

There is hope. Sometimes the manifestation of goodness and humanity – as demonstrated in Susan's voice – is so powerful that even the most unlikely people are pulled up sharp and, at least for a few moments, are confronted by qualities which are truly meaningful. If only people would hold on to this and not return to the pandering to the trivial. . .

I also rejoiced in John Sargent's popularity in 'Strictly Come Dancing'. It was so refreshing that personality gained more votes than oh-so-perfect displays which the contestants would probably have been taking oh-so-seriously.

* * *

How ludicrous and misguided can we get? I spotted a small news item. There was a photograph of a mother and her daughter who was about to celebrate her 21st birthday. Both women were attractive with good figures. The daughter, in particular, was very pretty.

The mother, it transpired, had already invested £45,000 in cosmetic surgery for herself and her gift to her beautiful young daughter was to pay for cosmetic surgery for her, too. My only hope was that it might be impossible to find a surgeon prepared to be guilty of such a sacrilege. Sadly, money talks.

This must illustrate how the effects of advertising, low self-esteem, too much money and no judgement on how it should be spent combine to do quite terrible damage. To me this ranked as child abuse, even if it took an unusual form.

* * *

In extreme cases the morbidly obese reach a point where they cannot even get out of bed, let alone out of the house. Where, then, does the food that they consume in great quantities come from?

Anyone who goes to the supermarket daily to keep the supply going is, to my mind, guilty of assault – possibly even of assisting, ultimately, suicide. This would be no better than a parent or partner procuring drugs in ever-increasing quantities in the full knowledge that in doing so he or she was likely to bring about the death of the other.

Where has natural common sense and a sense of responsibility gone? Where is genuine caring? A child who is loved is not bought a dozen ice creams on a day trip to the beach – just one or two, with the explanation that more will possibly make him feel ill, or spoil his appetite for tea.

* * *

Success – by being voted into Parliament, or getting to the top of a bank or large corporation – encourages those involved to believe themselves to be greatly superior to their fellow men. This attitude is strengthened by their subordinates, who often envy their wealth and position.

Celebrities fall into the same trap and many of them are not blessed with either intelligence or decency. They see themselves as entitled to an obscenely luxurious life-style even if the money runs out.

There was an amazing description of how one woman wanted to move into an (even bigger and better) house. She ordered every obscenely over-the-top item she could think of. Workmen did her bidding. Unfortunately for them their bill came to about £690,000 and woman had only £2,300 in the bank.

Are theses people with their multi-million pound homes content? In all probability they are not. They can be completely self-absorbed and hypercritical of the rest of the world. One very wealthy American woman complained to her neighbour – an English woman who was temporarily living next door because her husband had a job in the States – that she could hear ice cracking in the English woman's deep freezer when she was in her swimming pool. In the culture of find-any-reason-and-sue the English woman had to take this preposterous complaint seriously.

* * *

When the wealthy fall from grace and we are told have become insolvent I have often noted an apparent lack of change in their life-styles. In a just world I would have liked to see Robert Maxwell's family re-housed in the poor council flats that many decent people have to live in, and every penny of their personal wealth go to the pension funds of the employees he had robbed.

Is the reason this never happens because those in charge – politicians and the judiciary – line up so readily with the wealthy at the expense of the poor? Could they envisage a time when they could also be put in a position of disgrace, and they would certainly not wish to attract a humiliating punishment?

Blair scored a first. Neither John Major not any of his prime minister predecessors humiliated their country by begging free holidays for themselves and their families in exotic places from the rich and famous – but Tony did. I was relieved to see that after becoming Prime Minister Gordon Brown, his wife and sons, enjoyed the sandy beach of a British resort.

There were reports that as he left office Blair arranged for masses of papers to be shredded. I could not help wondering if his expenses claims had been among them.

* * *

The way in which the government dishes out money – our money, the tax-payers' money – gives a good indication of its mindset and the people with whom it identifies. In love with the wealthy – even if the wealthy happen to be bankers whose greed and incompetence reduced the country to bankruptcy – the prime minister, chancellor of the exchequer, etc., were not prepared even to cap the bonuses of those bankers – even though huge sums of public money had been used to keep their banks afloat.

However, when it came to saving Post Offices, which play an enormous part in the lives of ordinary people – and that is the problem, they are ordinary and can be ignored – no subsidy was offered to keep them open.

Every village must have a Post Office. Towns need a number – enough so that pensioners and everyone else can pop along to post a little birthday gift – which cannot be put in the post box – buy a few stamps, and pay many of the household bills. This can include buying vouchers towards bigger bills which are expected, an important consideration for those on small incomes who like to keep their affairs in order, another minority despised by the government.

Even more important is the part played by Post Offices in

the community, as they offer friendship and support. I knew of pensioners who wept when their local Post Office closed. A part of their lives had been wrenched from them. Where did their locally elected MPs stand? Interestingly, while he dealt sympathetically with correspondence from the vast numbers who opposed the closure, he thanked the sub-postmaster for agreeing to accept the package he had been offered for agreeing to close the business, saying that such co-operation made such closures possible for the government.

* * *

So – the government has its priorities. First it must squander billions and billions of pounds on wars the people did not support. (This was an investment necessary so that Blair would cosy up to the AMERICAN PRESIDENT! Pity that now many Americans see Bush as the worst president they ever had. . .) Then, next in the queue for the taxpayers' money are their wealthy cronies – some of whom may, with luck, make donations to the political parties – and who are, at the very least, their sort of people – and then there are things like the Post Office and the postmen who deliver the letters – little people of no consequence and with whom our mighty leaders have no intention of identifying in any way. Tough on the electorate, but the only say they have is once every five years when they have the choice of voting for one of a number of candidates most of whom are clones of each other.

* * *

Money, money, money. Cherie Blair was asked to confirm some time after her husband had left office whether their property portfolio amounted to £12,000,000 and she admitted that it did. However, she was quick to point our that there were only five homes involved, not six as was alleged. Confusion had arisen as two houses had been knocked into one.

I could not help thinking of Marie Antoinette, and 'Let them eat cake'. Cherie would not be beheaded, but in my opinion she had put her head in the moral noose.

How did they get so much money? A tiny part of it came from the sum of over £100,000 which Cherie demanded before agreeing to be the after dinner speaker at an event to raise money for a charity supporting children with cancer. When I heard about this I was mind blown. Some of my little criminals would have loved to work, free, to help these sick children. And what about Cherie's level of intelligence – would anyone really want to be seen to have made this demand? Publicity was also given to the fact that she charged more than most other barristers when carrying out work under legal aid funding. Poor taxpayers!

* * *

Are our leaders only surrounded by people like themselves? Thank goodness for the Daily Telegraph and the often-maligned 'investigative journalism'. Without this MPs would have been able to continue to rip off the electorate – taxpayers – with their highly dubious expenses system, which had been designed by themselves for themselves (wouldn't a lot of us like that sort of arrangement!) and all sorts of bare-faced cheating which went along with it.

Actually, there are sometimes good people who have access to those at the top – but are unlikely to remain in work if they fail to say what the leaders wish them to.

Some time before the disastrous state of the banks' finances became public knowledge one man did approach Gordon Brown. He had foreseen disaster, and warned him what was taking place and what was going to happen unless quick and drastic action was taken. He was fired.

It is a generally accepted fact that while Westminster was reeling under the weight of the expenses scandal corruption and fraud – and even more inflated expenses – were being dished out to representatives in the European Economic Community. Similarly one brave fellow expressed his concerns to Neil Kinnock, and he also lost his job.

In June 2010 there was a report that Neil's son Stephen was facing allegations of tax evasion in Denmark, where his wife was leader of the country's opposition, the Social Democrats.

When it became obvious that there would be public pressure on members of the House of Commons to cut back on their expenses Gordon Brown soon suggested that the same SISO (sign in and sod off) system should come into force in Westminster which was already in place in Brussels. At the start of the day representatives signed in. Whether they remained or not did not matter – they collected a big daily allowance in addition to their already large salaries. By a round-about route he got his way. In July 2009 it became known that MPs could claim £25 – no receipts needed – for a night away from home on parliamentary business. But it had to be £25. One member had the option – his travel to and from his constituency cost £8 – of overcharging or putting in the claim one night in three. But this would have provided records that showed – wrongly – that he had only spent a third of his time with his constituents. . .

* * *

Just imagine if the rest of us – those that have to clock in and out because we are on flexi-time or whatever – only had to clock in. . . ! and that this entitled us to extra money in addition to our pay packets! Wow!

So while Brown's SISO was not incorporated a system was installed by which an additional £9,125 allowance could be had annually. This arrangement was agreed after the new Speaker of the House, John Bercow, more loved by Labour than his fellow Conservatives, had been sworn in replacing

Michael Martin. Is it surprising that cynics say, 'Nothing ever changes'?

* * *

Hearteningly the public, Mr and Mrs Reasonable Average, can and sometimes do change. Those who had played it a bit fast and loose financially – I am not talking about the ones who overspent disastrously – did tighten their belts. Statistics showed that there was a move afoot to repay their mortgages. Most of us are realists and can behave responsibly.

Can we now hope for a more responsible government? The book was written during the Blair/Brown era. I now want to add a few observations. The advent of a coalition government may – and I hope it will – mean that there is some genuine debate on all subjects, with extreme views having no chance of materialising as policies. The gross deficit the coalition inherited must be taken seriously, and the country must be sympathetic when nasty measures have to be taken as the country tries to get back to balancing its books.

Ed Miliband has just been elected as Labour Party Leader. He has declared – very belatedly, in my opinion, that he believes the war against Iraq was wrong. So late did he let this view become common knowledge that I find myself wondering whether he kept quiet so as not to damage his earlier political opportunities, but is now seeing his stance as politically advantageous. However, while noting this with some concern, the position now is that two out of three political party leaders are openly hostile to the disastrous Iraq war, which delights me. Blair – waving the war-mongering flag – has said on more than one occasioion that 'we' might have to do the same thing in Iran that we did in Iraq. Hopefully the political balance in our country now means that this could not be contemplated. Please let us now have a decent and responsible government.

* * *

Behaving responsibly is certainly not what bankers did or intend to do in the future. Aided by their mates in Brown's government – who were not prepared to impose tough rules unlike the American authorities – the arrogant and greedy in the banking trade clung on to their obscenely large incomes and bonuses.

I found it mind-blowing that the argument that if these people – who had proved totally incompetent in managing their banks' and the country's finances – had to take a pay cut we would 'lose the top talent' in the banking industry. What 'top talent' – they had proved themselves a liability, not an asset. Pack them off abroad by all means. Jo Public certainly does not want them here.

A former chief executive of one bank had earned £4.2 million a year and left with a £16.6 million pension pot. Lest he be seen in the wrong light he gave the assurance (modestly) that 200 of his staff earned more that he did. . .

* * *

More and more there is evidence that those perceiving themselves to be on high have lost all sense of humanity and decency. Very poorly paid council workers were actually expected to take cuts as a result of the depression. These people, on the whole and unlike the bankers, do their jobs properly. Everyone would soon protest if rubbish was not removed from the streets or there were no ladies to dish out school meals.

* * *

There is a sad spin-off as a result of media perception of important and unimportant people. Children tend to get tarred with the same brush as their parents.

Contrast the interest and concern shown when Madeline McCann went missing with that for Shannon Matthews. One family, expensive professionals, achieved massive publicity. They even set up some sort of search fund used, in part, to help with their mortgage. The child was pretty.

Shannon Matthews – poor little scrap – had a tragically inadequate family. Her mother loved her so much that she was made the victim of a plot to raise money from her 'kidnapping'. In fact, the greater concern could have been for Shannon, who had never known stability or comfort, rather that the indulged life which had been enjoyed by Madeline. One had, at least, known happiness and love, the other misery and suffering.

CONCLUSION

I have invited you to 'Heal Society'. Much of what I have written may appear to indicate that such an aim is impossible to achieve - but is this the case? In defining 'society' I hope we can come to a more optimistic conclusion.

What is society? I am society, you are society, and the individuals around us are society. Society is not some anonymous block. In the same way that a honeycomb exists only because of each individual cell so there would be no society if it were not for each and every one of us. We are society, and society is us. Politicians and bureaucrats would suppress this fact. We are the 'little people' of no account other than to do their bidding, and to be the butt of their blame and criticisms if things go wrong. It is our role, in their eyes, to slot into the patterns they have created for us.

More fool us if we conform! It is up to us to have the strength of our own convictions, as individuals, and lead the lives which we want and know to be right and proper. While we are besieged by news items reported in the media, in fact our immediate lives are affected by these events relatively infrequently, or to a very small degree. Our awareness is largely confined to what is happening around us. This being the case, how we and those in our immediate environment behave defines the state of society. Taken that we and our groups are inter-dependent, and that the people in all these groups overlap and interlink with other groups, it can be seen that we form an immensely powerful force - the body which is, in reality, society.

Of course we cannot force other people to behave well or share our good motivation. But many can be won over, or at least persuaded to take a fresh look at what life is all about. There is no magic here. All we have to do is to encourage them to get back in touch with their own humanity - the innate goodness which is in all, and which if recognized and acknowledged for what it is will bring about a healing both for the individual and for society at large.

At one level - and the one most easily achievable - it is possible to exert a hugely beneficial influence on the environment immediately around us - and not to underestimate that the effect of this is like ripples on a pond, travelling ever outwards for the greater benefit.

We should also give some measure of priority to trying to influence those who have apparent power, MPs, local councilors, the governors of schools, etc. and not allow ourselves to abandon our cause if our suggestions, ideas, and criticisms are met with a cool response. We must not get discouraged or angry - ideally just keep plugging away and hopefully find other like-minded people to support us. We must do what we can, and avoid becoming defeatist no matter what the circumstances. I know this is easier said than done.

One word of advice. Before getting heavily into any cause stand back and check if it has the virtue of enhancing the expression of humanity for those concerned. All too often people become obsessed with causes and situations which are far too partisan in their aims and would potentially be of limited benefit to a small group of people sometimes at the expense of others. Make sure what you are fighting for is really worth-while. Knowing that right is on your side gives you limitless strength.

Tread wearily if you find opposition appears to have good and well-reasoned arguments. It may be that then your role would be to work towards a compromise. Always keep an open mind - this is how we all learn! And don't mind if you sometimes have to admit that your first ideas or reactions were wrong. We develop, situations develop, and nothing in this life is static.

At all times and in all situations apply the acid test - is what I am doing going to benefit humanity? If the answer is 'Yes go for it and if not hold back - your energy can be used more profitably elsewhere

Thank you for reading this book. If you are already one of those whose motivation and wishes are to heal society be assured that we, the silent majority, are right behind you.

If you were in doubt as to whether such an aim was worth pursuing I hope I have been able to convince you. If not, please keep thinking about it. It is never too late to join the club!

My love and best wishes to you all,

Alison

I ask in the name of Jesus Christ
and god Almighty, the highest
Angels and Council of Elders —to
remove the energies of all
old habits and beliefs that
were instilled in me by an imposter
outside force, source;
I ask that all images I hold
of myself and unwanted
desires that do not belong
to me be released. I
ask to be cleansed of all
negative energies, hindering
habits and beliefs so
that I may serve my life
purpose.
I am ready to begin a
new life in a new way
in a way god intented
~~see~~ ~~does~~.
I ask to be my True
Self, the pure self that
I came into this
world with, be cleansed
and renewed in power
and purpose. And

So it is. It is so.

Juice oranges 8-9, one pomegrante
and 2 passion fruits. —

28 Day Folicing Kickstart Program.

Base   100g roasted Hazenuts
       250 s Soaked dates
       250g Almond meal
       40 g Cacao powder
       30 g melted Coconut oil.

Blend all ingred in food processor
except for hazelnuts then fold
them Into a mixture Smooth
mixture into a loaf pan
chocolate icing
100 g roasted Hazelnuts
20 g   Cacao
50 g   Agrave
20 g   Coconut oil
Blend hazelnuts until a
butter form   Add remaining
 Ingred Scraping down sides
of bowl   add a small amout
of water slowly with mixer
running until a good icing
consistency is formed. Spread
onto and refrigerate until
   set about 30 mins cut